RUN IT!

GEORGIA VARJAS

By The Author School

Published in Great Britain by ink! By The Author School 2020
Text © Georgia Varjas 2020
Cover Design © Helen Braid 2020

A CIP catalogue for this book is available from the British
Library.

ISBN 978-1-5272-5768-9

Typeset in Arial 11/14 by Blaze Typesetting

Printed in Great Britain by Clays Ltd, Elcograf S.p.A.

By The Author School
ink! By The Author School
Kent, England, United Kingdom
Email: info@hashtagpress.co.uk
Website: www.ink publishingservices.co.uk
Twitter: @services_ink

Denise Roberts, Founder of The Editor's Chair and Lunch and Learn for First-Time Authors

The fact that you are here thinking about reading this book makes me exceedingly happy for you. You are in for a real treat. *Rule It!* by Georgia Varjas is not a book you read and forget about on your bookshelf. It's the kind you keep close by—for those inevitable moments when you know you need a stiff talking to, a kick up the rear end, that kind of straight-talking, soul-reviving rebuke you know you've got coming when you're not doing what you know you should be doing to Step Up & Stand Out.

I wanted to get up out of my chair, dust off my blue suede shoes and rediscover my strut. Quite literally.

And that's what I love about this book. It's as if Georgia's discovered some secret passage to the backdoor of your self-doubts, waltzed right in and injected you with an antidote.

To what?

Well, the problem many of us women face is that we're overdosed on what Georgia calls the Three Little Cs—Cooking, Cleaning and Caring—and lacking in what she calls the Three Big Cs—Courage, Confidence and Creativity. We self-sabotage. We are our own worst enemies. As Georgia argues, *"Stopping ourselves from achieving what we want in life and business has become a serious malady. It gets to the point where the stories we are telling ourselves have more relevance and influence on our success than any external obstacle could ever do to us."*

Good news: our fears are 'powered by our own glorious imaginations', which means we have the ability to do something about them. That's what the book will help you to do.

It will help you to liberate your courage from its often narrow association 'with physical acts of strength' and to view other deeds of bravery women tend to excel at, like raising children while working part-time, quitting a well-paid job to start a business and standing on stage to tell your personal story—aren't these all also brave acts?

The book encourages us to pinpoint our confidence-sappers, but not to 'over-analyse, overthink or over-label them', and discusses the important link between creativity, confidence and courage: *"Being creative gives us confidence to explore and express, and urges us to take action—and that is courage."*

Georgia wraps her commonsense advice in brilliant one-liners, metaphors and mental surprises. . . telling us to get off the 'Con Belt' (conveyor belt) of life, steer clear of 'comparison-itis' and know our strong points—the special talents, skills and things we excel at and love to do—so as to start *'the courage-pot boiling'*.

Stage dominance won't come overnight, Georgia tells us. It takes work. It takes making mistakes and learning from them. But we can rest knowing that in this book is the Courage, Confidence and Creativity to help us to get there.

Natalie Smith, Virtual Assistant / Business Owner
As a woman in my mid-thirties I recently had a bit of a mid-career/life crisis. After having children, being beaten down by over a decade in the corporate world, and with ambitions to be my own boss and work on my own terms, I made the decision to change, but it's not been easy. As part of this quest to change my life, I have opened up to learning new skills, embracing personal development and recognising the need to invest in myself.
I have read A LOT of books, some resonating with me more than others, some more useful than others, but I can honestly say that 'Rule It' really struck a chord with me and opened my eyes to not just the 'why' things have previously been difficult for women like me, but with practical suggestions of 'how' to move past it and thrive in life going forward.

This book has made me realise and face the fears,

obstacles, habits and beliefs that I can now see have been holding me back my whole life.

A particular ah ha moment was reading about what Georgia calls the Three little Cs (cooking, cleaning and caring). This is what I've always referred to as my 'mental load'. Even though I consider myself a modern career woman, working mum, multitasker, equality at home—even I outsource or share some of the traditional tasks associated with the Three Little Cs let's face it, it's usually the woman who has to organise the outsourcing, plan who's going to do what and when and does most of the 'caring' about the people and the duties of the family and takes the responsibility of the 'adulting' and 'admin' within the household.

It's no wonder that there's not enough headspace to get good at the Three Big Cs—Confidence, Courage and Creativity!

Rule It! Has made me understand the reasons behind some of my lack of confidence and given me practical ways to get better about stepping up, putting myself and my work out there!

It's a must read for women at all stages of their lives, careers or business. I'll be dipping in and out when I need some inspiration and motivation!

*To giving women and girls a pen and a voice
to Step Up & Stand Out so they can Rule It!*

CONTENTS

CONTENTS

FOREWORD

As I type this, I hear the giggles of my nine-month-old in the background as he plays with his sisters. But running a writing business while baby-wrangling is hard. Sometimes my battery is down to zero. What's left for me? How do I keep the spark alive for my writing? Where do I take my business next?

That's when I turn to *Rule It!* In these pages Georgia serves a powerful and timely reminder that we all have tools at our disposal to get life and work buzzing again. She calls them the Three Big Cs. She shows us how nurturing these three and putting them into action is game-changing, both in terms of our mindset and our success out there in the big wide world.

We all have times when it feels too much. When our hearts tremble at the distance between the writer/performer/speaker we want to be and where we are now, or our shoulders sag with the certainty our best work is behind us. Georgia reminds us we've all been there—we're not alone when we're down. We don't have to stay there. She shows us how to turn setbacks into opportunities, and how to create new networks when existing ones say "No thanks." More than anything, this book is a reminder that there is always a choice—always a way forward.

As women, we are so often told, explicitly or implicitly, to sit down, be nice, shut up, put up, enjoy the scraps we might be offered. Georgia's having none of it. She wants us to dream big and walk tall. No waiting around to be invited in, she wants us to bust the wall down, say our piece and say it proud. She shows us how. And, importantly, she reminds us that in doing so, we pave the way for other women to use their voices too. And, heavens alive, the world needs more of that right now.

Rule It! is a long drink of iced lemon water in a time of drought. It's zingy, refreshing, and exactly what you need to jump into action when you're feeling woozy or uncertain. It's time to stop waiting to be asked. It's time to stop holding yourself back. It's time to get yourself on the stage, page or wherever you want to be. . . and Rule It!

Gayle Johnson
Copywriter and writing mentor
www.redtreewriting.com

INTRODUCTION

Rule It!—How To Step Up & Stand Out
On Video, Stage & Page

After I finished writing *The Rule Breaker's Guide*, I knew I had more to say on the subject of Stepping Up & Standing Out. I also knew it had to be in another volume. I wanted to offer my readers specifics: how to get down to the nitty gritty of what holds us back, what prevents so many talented women and men from expressing themselves in a way that educates, entertains and uplifts—and most importantly—provides financial rewards.

In *The Rule Breaker's Guide*, I wrote about the importance of being authentic and courageously stepping off the Con Belt (Conveyer Belt) of life. I wrote about believing in yourself, being consistent, persistent, resistant and insistent. I wrote about the trials and tribulations of being female in male-dominated professions. How you had to be twice as good and always professional. I touched on professional jealousy, appearance, and the tricky mire of being or not being sexy. I talked about the pain, insult and downgrading of not being heard, understood or believed. I discussed the glass ceiling, with and without cracks. I covered a lot of topics.

And now, I want to offer more solutions and practical actions about how to scatter your talents to the four corners and still look good! To detail the most common obstacles that hold many of us back, so you can see how to manoeuvre around them. How you can dismiss and dismantle them and use your awareness of those barriers and limitations you still have lurking, to kick them off your planet. This book is about the tools and tips from my lifetime in showbiz as a writer, playwright, musician, performance poet, speaker and author.

The world stage is open to everyone.

It is possible for every one of us to appear on video, stage and page. We are watching people from all walks of life making videos on Facebook, Instagram (IG), Pinterest, LinkedIn and Twitter. Writing articles, selling their products and services, sharing their stories, opinions and images of their stories, opinions and lives. The world is the stage and at some point we all have a chance to jump on it. Shakespeare made that clear some centuries ago.

> *"If all the world is a stage, I suggest you start performing at your best."*
> Rob Liano - author and speaker

With so many doors open and so many opportunities available, it conjures up an image that each of us can become successful writers, speakers, spoken word artists, story performers and entrepreneurs—if not overnight then pretty quickly! And why not?

With that attitude you must succeed—right?

Unfortunately, it takes time, perseverance, investment, character and a little luck—being in the 'right place at the right time' kind of luck. It also takes hard work, consistency and a huge ability to:

> *"Turn your obstacles into opportunities*
> *and your problems into possibilities."*
> Roy T Bennett - author

And as we all know, obstacles, hurdles and difficulties are everywhere, both externally and in our heads!

What's in a Word?

Regrettably, disparity, discrimination and imbalances are highlighted every day in the news, on social media and in our homes. And we know it is heavily tilted against females (even that word does not distinguish us with clarity; the *fe* is connected to the *male*, as is the *wo* fixed to the *man*).

Emphasis on the power of language is in many articles

and books, yet little is mentioned of the awareness of the damage, the stains and stigmas it has on more than half the population—women. There are people of all ages who feel nervous at having a woman pilot, scared to have a female president, anxious that the surgeon is a woman.

The bias and injustice towards women are still excessive. Laws have created the first steps to redress this, but not enough of them have been implemented.

For female writers, speakers, word and story artists, and entrepreneurs, the struggle to gain payment for services and products increases. Proving your value and standing up to the ingrained bias against women play havoc with our confidence, courage and creativity.

There Are No Rules to Reading *Rule It!*
In this book, I aim to provide steps, moves and changes that you can implement from today. A book you can dip in and out of as you need. So, if one day you feel you need some encouragement to get up, take action and put your decision into play, there will be a chapter to boost and support you.

If you need to develop more confidence, there will be a chapter to energise and excite you, to grab hold of some attitude and feel more confident. And if you need a quick boost, turn to Georgia's Gems on page 128.

You may want to read *Rule It!* from cover to cover and

lay it on the table for others to read, as you leap around exhilarated and psyched up to promote and celebrate your own work.

In our world today, people want to know more about the person behind that book, article, brand or video. Our curiosity for information is growing and evolving. There is a natural human inquisitiveness to discover more about the author, the speaker, the amazing story performance you saw on YouTube or at a TEDx event.

By developing your creative energy and having the confidence and courage to be visible—to show yourself out there on the world stage—you up-level your profile, your reputation and your chances of gaining financial rewards for your work.

This book is all about showing you how to Step Up & Stand Out on Video, Stage and Page. It is about recognising the obstacles that are holding you back and learning how to expel, release and disown them. It is about re-defining what courage is for you and teaming it up with your new exuberant confidence and your amazing creative skills to make a life and business that works for you.

When you acknowledge the numerous subtle and blatant biases that prevent you from displaying your true genius, you will want to release that fire and channel it into succeeding and achieving what you want.

It is a roller coaster ride.
It will be tough and challenge you.
And make you wanna cry, curse and laugh!

But let's face it, are you going to give up?
Put your exquisite tools down and walk out?
Let your genius blow in the wind?

No way! Because let's face it—we do want more!
We want to *Rule It!*

CHAPTER ONE

Obstacles of the Stubborn Kind

The word out there is that if you really want something in life, all you have to do is go for it. Decide, prepare and head on out there and grab it.

It's a brilliant idea and a great attitude to have. Unfortunately, the 'road to achievement and success' is not a straight line or a level playing field. Mountains, deep ravines and all kinds of gates and fences pepper that path to the flourishing and nourishing life we seek.

Some of those obstacles are easier to overcome with persistence and verve. For others you will need influence, money and connections—or nepotism in some professions—while others may appear small but are really icebergs. There are rules and guidelines and you will need entry tickets, passports and money to get in. Yes, you could say obstacles are everywhere and represent both challenges and opportunities. And that is certainly the frame of mind to have as a writer, speaker or business owner.

The rules are not always what they seem. They are often one thing on paper and another in practice. They can open doors or slam them in your face. It is up to you to question and challenge when rules are used against you or provide no benefit.

It has to be stated early on that the hurdles and obstacles that women have to jump over are intrinsically different from most men. And for women facing these external obstacles, it's all too easy to internalise them and create our own obstacles too—but more on that in the next chapter. As speakers, writers and entrepreneurs, we are not immune from gender inequality. In fact, in some ways, we're uniquely placed to both experience it and call it out.

And whether you accept this gender bias, cannot see it or deny it—I know it exists, and this cartoon is the perfect illustration.[1]

The Three Cs of Womanhood

When I was 20, a business friend was shocked and horrified to learn that I hadn't had secretarial training. He couldn't believe I couldn't type or do shorthand. It was a skill every female should have, he firmly believed.

I was labelled and stamped as 'useless' with slim

prospects of finding any work because I could not type, nurse or care. In fact, his exact words were, "A woman who can't type is like a woman with one leg!"

A woman is expected to cook, clean and care. What I call the three most undervalued and underpaid jobs in the world. It is no surprise to learn that most of the cooking, cleaning and caring worldwide (and throughout history) is performed by women.

But wait, before you tell me you don't do the Three Little Cs, that your husband does, you have a cleaner, you can't cook and you don't care for anyone. . . think again.

If we observe the way men live, often with no or little obligation, responsibility or requirement to cook, clean and care, and heavy praise when they do (think about how gooey everyone gets about men cuddling babies, or simply being a parent!), disproportionate asymmetry becomes clear.

It is so deeply ingrained in our DNA from centuries and ongoing perpetuation that the three hugely time-consuming tasks of cooking, cleaning and caring are carried out by women.

Most men seldom have to consider who will cook, clean or care for them, or for their mothers, grandparents and even their own children. This is 'women's work'. Let's face it, women have always done it.

There is a hazy line regarding the way a woman performs or does not perform these Three Little Cs. Judgement and assumptions are present. . . and punishments too. The stigma surrounding women who do not cook, clean or care still abounds. You are a 'bad mother' or 'not a proper woman' if you don't. Yet, seldom are men scolded or criticised for not doing these tasks. Of course, many women rebel—they don't cook, refuse to care and never clean. But they are not respected for it.

For those women who cook, clean and care for children or family members and have to work (and many are in low paid jobs to fit in with all the cooking, cleaning and caring they are obliged to do) they know they will have to face down some serious obstructions, restrictions and stumbling blocks if they want to jump up on stage, create a video or find time to write that book.

Women need to share the burden of the Three Little Cs. Why? Well, basic fairness for one thing. There is nothing in a man's brain or body that means he is not equipped to whisk an egg, clean a bathroom or wipe a baby's bottom any less than a woman. Yet, if women spend all their energy on the Three Little Cs, it means there's no time for anything else. This book is all about the Three Big Cs, the life-changing ones:

Courage, Creativity and Confidence. We need to shift our attention from always doing the Three Little Cs to let the magnificent three in.

She Works Hard for the Money

As Donna Summer sang back in 1983, *"She works hard for the money."*[2]

Women often work 2 or 3 jobs and then come home to do the Three Little Cs.[3] If you're one of these women then balancing the Three Little Cs with the Three Big Cs may leave you looking frazzled. If you're a single woman you may not experience it but every blog, article and a whole number of videos are talking about self-care. So, maybe it does affect you after all.

The Gender Pay Gap is increasingly hitting the news. Receiving pay equality clearly has an immense effect on increasing our options and investing in ourselves. Education and care costs money. Being recognised, valued and credited for our work increases our confidence, courage and creativity.

In 1963, The Equal Pay Act was signed into law in the United States of America. In the United Kingdom it was made law in 1970, Australia in 1969, and Canada in 1956. Yet women still receive unequal pay in these countries varying from 18% to 34% less than men. The global figures still show significant discrepancies. When women take pay discrimination cases to court, there are few positive results. Secrecy, lack of transparency and deeply ingrained unconscious gender bias cover most of the reasons for this continuing inequality in pay.

You think it doesn't happen in your world? You think female authors, journalists, actors and speakers are treated and paid the same as male counterparts? Do you think it doesn't have an impact on your confidence, courage and creativity?

Let me share one story. Lhakpa Sherpa works for minimum wages and currently washes dishes, as she trains for her tenth Everest summit with no endorsement deals, no nutritionist and no trainer.[4]

With a lack of sponsorship, lack of recognition and lack of finances, she still plans her 10th climb in 2020 and says: "I want to show the world I can do it. I want to show women who look like me that they can do it, too."

Many people think or have convinced themselves that things have changed but similar stories are still being shared.[5] That women and men are equal. That the gap is shrinking. Women can do everything that men do. Except they get paid less, are seldom credited or rewarded, hardly recognised and rarely climb to the top as CEOs, effective politicians or representatives of power. And they are expected to handle the Three Little Cs as well.

- If you are male, these are the jobs, tasks and lifestyle you should lead.
- If you are a woman, make sure you cook, clean and care and **then** these are the jobs, tasks and lifestyle you should lead.

And men are affected by stereotyping too—they still cannot openly be 'good' fathers without paying social, cultural and financial penalties. Expectations about successful male behaviour is still centred around physical prowess, mental abilities and the power of the dollar/euro/yen in his pocket.

My point being—obstacles abound. They are written in our DNA, what is now accepted as 'unconscious bias'. It is stamped on that sneaky pre-birth gender planning that parents create, aided and abetted by society. It is clearly defined in most areas of life that we touch upon, from birth to death.

A woman does this in life. She is nice, she breeds, she is still nice, she nurtures and educates all males and some females. She remains nice. She performs the Three Cs (Cook, Clean and Care), remains nice and takes very little credit, recognition or reward for any of it. If she does, she is a bitch, show-off, whore, slag, cheat, fake. . .

A man, on the other hand, has a much freer reign of the land and himself. The laws are stacked for him.

Aggressive, 'wild oats' behaviour is admired. Penalties are few and far between, as they are perpetrated most skilfully by men in higher positions (who incidentally make and break their own rules).

A man must fulfil. . . whatever he pleases. However, this only apples to men who fit neatly within certain criteria:

- Being white, that is Western white.
- Preferably from class and or money.
- Powerful ancestors with titles and money.

If you tick these boxes, there's little you can't get away with. Any signs of fraud, coercion, bestiality, torture, rape of minors, or other kinds of bad behaviour must be carefully and secretly hidden, and it happens.

Men suffer under a misogyny too. The 'man-up' culture holds strong with suicide and gang warmongering, killing men and boys in ever increasing numbers yearly. Men would benefit from opening up, connecting, and playing more of a part in the Three Cs world.

But back to women. The punishment that women receive for stepping out of line, rebelling against the system (or any man) are harsh, and far worse, as they are carried out often without any legal or medical dispute or resistance.

Fighting back carries heavy penalties for a woman. Stepping out of your comfort zone may bring you great benefits but can also piss a lot of people off—both women and men.

Our world is full of prejudice, inherited judgements and vengeful assumptions. Some are deeply stained on our psyche and others we bat around thoughtlessly. And unfortunately, some are still written in stone. But stones can be broken, cracked and removed—there is hope!

Working in an Unfair World

During my days in the music world, I played alto saxophone, and I was constantly being reminded to dress, look and "behave like a girl". If my hair was messy, I was criticised for being ungroomed. If my hair was combed I was told to "Relax, be sexy!" It was annoying and infuriating that my job was not to play saxophone but to please the other players in the band.

Call it the glass ceiling, the bamboo floor or a concrete wall, excluding women from better paid, worthwhile and reputable positions still goes on. Sometimes the obstacles are subtle, like quips about your appearance. Sometimes they are blindingly obvious, like shameful pay differences.

These obstacles are damaging. They deter, derail and demean your ability and value. They can put you off and stop you in your tracks if you are not determined enough, or if you don't have the right back up or financial resources.

There are still hang-ups about placing women in so called 'traditional male' jobs. Just ask the military, judicial system or neuroscience. Never mind senior roles in government or CEOs of global companies.

Perhaps we need to investigate why so few men are nursery teachers or work as midwives? Why do fathers have such a hard time taking paternity leave? The statistics are out there. Several authors have put the evidence down in writing. Yet we doubt and shrug and say, "Not any more, surely?"

Tactics of the most subversive kind are installed at every corner, as former BBC China Editor, Carrie Gracie, outlines in her book, *Equal*.[6] And lack of money is at the root of all female dependence. With financial independence and support, women can have an effect on their outcomes.

It is clear that being recognised and financially rewarded for your work and your contributions are of vital importance to your mental health, never mind your physical state of living.

And the stakes get higher the more children you have, the more dependents you are responsible for: ageing parents, sick babies, unwell children. Try doing that without another bread winner and immediately your troubles are doubled. Then there are huge differences if your class, race and religion do not fit in with the current political and social favours. Have a disability? You can stack up more disadvantages. Keep women poor and heavily burdened, then you will keep them down.

All these negative belief systems play havoc with our confidence and wellbeing. If we feel under-valued and belittled, how can we rise up and take on another task, another job? How can we step forward and ask for better conditions, or a pay rise, if we are not taken for our value and worth?

If this has been your experience, or that of other females around you, then it is hard to be strong and fight back, to say 'I can do this'.

How can a woman step up on stage and give an inspirational speech if she feels no one is listening, or no one will believe her, or even understanding her point of view?

How can you run a business and call it your own if you have no money to invest, no credit to your name or no experience behind you?

Or, if you want to write a book about your experiences, your point of view, or your journey, how are you going to get that book out there when publishers, editors and journalists favour the male name and the male version of life?

These obstacles are real and persistent. They can destroy your ambition and drive.

For a woman ready to branch out, spread her wings and make a go of her talents and skills, there are plenty of tricky hurdles and obstructions out there to veer you off track or back into your safe comfort zone (where you belong, of course).

In 2017, there was the Harvey Weinstein case, in which eighty women came forward telling their story of sexual abuse committed by this film tyrant. Yet, still nothing has been settled. If they don't believe eighty women, what then? What more is needed? Are all eighty women lying?[7]

We all believed situations such as the Harvey Weinstein case would be a massive wake-up call for men to start behaving properly! But a backlash has now evolved. Nasty and subversive as it is, men are now supporting the abusive film mogul. Men in powerful positions are belittling the word of eighty women, downgrading their abilities, their reputations and credit.

All of this carries a strong message and, in many cases, full-on punishment.

Back off, back down and shut up.

I have been dismissed from bands for not dressing right, not sleeping with the boss and not doing as I was told.

In the spoken word scene I have had my microphone sabotaged so my work was not heard, my performance denied and my name taken off the performers list. Why? Because I wasn't male. Well, actually, because I was a stroppy female. Translated as someone who spoke up, spoke back and refused to be pushed around.

Once at the Poetry Club in London's Covent Garden on an Open Mic night, there was a group of men (so called fellow poets) sitting in the front row, who talked loud and clear as soon as I began my set.

I tried a few of my 'shut the hecklers up' tricks, such as "Want to go to the toilet and continue the gossip?" But they just raised their voices. The host turned his back when I waved him down and so my three super-hot poems, well-rehearsed and dynamic, did not reach anyone's ears that night. Later, when I approached the host, he said, "Oh sorry, I didn't see it."

Sorry can be such an empty word. If the host and the front row boys are shutting you out why would you want to go back? I felt like going back with half a dozen Vikings and three Sumo wrestlers, but that was just a dream.

Facing down the host alone is—and was—pointless. If no one backs you up what can you do?

1. Make sure your friends and supporters are sitting in the front row.

2. Try and talk to the host beforehand to ask if he can keep an eye on any noisy audience members.

3. Approach the 'troublemakers' beforehand, chat to them, see how they behave when you are not reciting your work. If they behave the same, i.e. ignore you, go back to number 2.

4. Find another venue that offers more respect to spoken word artists.

5. Write an article damming them, tweet about them, take a photo of them to use on social media. Women do not have to be nice.

Dress to Impress

One of the most humiliating things that happen to women on stage and screen is the critique and commentary about their outfit, hair and physical shape and size. Yes, bullies are everywhere and come in both female and male frames. But the rules about what women wear and how big, small or sexy they are, create enormous and gratuitous attention.

The list of misdemeanours is long, exhausting and truly insulting. It is not only your size, but the number of bulges you have, and how you cover them or expose them.

- "Your clothes are too revealing/too frumpy."
- "You are showing off by wearing this outfit."

- "You are too old to be wearing that dress."
- "Your legs are too fat/big/skinny/knobbly for the length of your dress."
- "Why are you showing so much cleavage?"

The array of critical comments about a woman's appearance on stage or screen is endless. A man stands up on stage and he is either handsome, ugly or old. His clothes are smart or casual and that is it! He is wearing a T-shirt? Well, that's OK. He is in a suit? Well, that's OK too. Actually, who cares?

Honestly, every time I have come off stage after a speech, spoken word performance, even as an MC, the first comments are about my appearance.

- "You shouldn't wear black."
- "You mustn't wear jewellery."
- "Those shoes are noisy."
- "Your hair is messy."
- "You need some make-up."
- "Can you take off that jacket, it's too loud!"

Seldom has the first comment been: "Fabulous! What an inspiration you are!"

I went for numerous auditions when I was a saxophone player. I always intend to dress to impress. I do know and believe that if you look your best (in your opinion) that is enough. Dressing up for an audition where you know you are going to meet a bunch of male musicians is tricky, I admit.

Dress too flash, too flamboyant and you may frighten them off. Wearing a pair of jeans and T-shirt i.e. dressing like a man, is risky too. If the jeans are too tight and your T-shirt too—well, hell you could be creating a false impression!

In fact, tight sexy clothing will create a stir and a ruffle between the boys. Bad start. You don't want them vying for you and competing with each other, do you? Dress down and cover your assets, and they will dismiss you pretty quickly as not being suitable for an upcoming band or indeed help their style and reputation. Work that one out? I am still searching for the logic in that.

I have been in a band where the band leader asked me first, that is before **even** hearing me play my instrument, to put on an item of clothing that was basically lingerie.

I have been asked to wear ridiculous high heels while playing my instrument (totally putting my body balance out). I have been advised to wear a sexy top and a short skirt on stage otherwise the audience won't be able to see I am a girl. I have been advised by a band leader to not play in certain songs and just dance sexy instead.

Not knowing what to wear to please the person in command (who can give you the speaking slot or spot) can ruin your confidence, dampen your resolve and really put you off going for it.

Too many of us women spend heaps of time fussing over our appearance before, during and after our time on stage and screen. We do the dreaded three over-the-top things:

1. We over-think.
2. We over-analyse.
3. We over-label.

And sadly, we do it in many areas of our lives. Believe me, perfectionism is a confidence killer. Worrying about your appearance can set you back years. Anxiety about how you look can stop your ambition. And labelling yourself as too fat/thin/old/young/ugly etc can deter you for a lifetime.

These are serious obstacles that can easily almost unnoticeably become internalised and damaging for life. But more on that in the next chapter.

How do you deal with or handle blatant or subtle sexism, misogyny and double standards?

How can you face up to the brick wall of successful entry into life that oozes of a Boys' Club mentality?

Shame that in the 2020s, women and girls from all races and religions still have this dilemma. But we do. So, what can we do about it?

The What To Do List
Here is my list of things you can do to tackle brick walls, misogyny, sexism and outright discrimination, when you work on video, stage and page. In no particular order:

- Don't beat yourself up. It has happened to millions of women for thousands of years. Recognise it—accept it—be aware of it. It still exists. And it's not worth punishing yourself for something you did not design or inflict.
- Dust off your bruises and knock backs. Never give up—re-invent yourself. Team up, collaborate with other like-minded women. Look for solutions rather than harping on the problem. Start your own writers' group, spoken word club night, or Facebook group to share concerns, advice and solutions.
- Check out your mistakes and see them as feedback. It's not about who is to blame but what you can take forward with you. And what you can avoid or not repeat.
- Disarm your critics. Find your way to disarm,

dismiss and deactivate your critics, enemies, opposites and competition. I know it is easy to say and harder to do when someone is bad-mouthing you or your work. I know because it happened to me enough times. I learnt to say, "Thank you for your comments." And walk away. I learnt to listen, smile and move on. I learnt not to waste my anger on someone else's opinion.

- Keep learning. Stimulate your creative side. Watch/see/read about artists, dancers, actors, authors and speakers. Keep whetting your appetite.
- Work on your Power of Words. Expand your language skills with writing and reading. Learn another language. Put some creases in your thesaurus. Spark up your vocabulary through sharpening your listening skills.
- Always find time for *Numero Uno*! Remember, if YOU ain't got your health—well you ain't got your wealth. And vice versa. Make time to enjoy life and do things just for you. This is especially true if you find yourself doing the Three Little Cs all too often.
- Don't take yourself so seriously. Learn to laugh. Look for the funny side. Take a breath, curse, cry and scream—and then laugh. As often as you can.
- Be professional, not perfect. Utilise your passion,

personality and performance to drive you, keep you determined and fuel your energy. We will talk more about how to do this later on in the book.

- Don't get angry—get money. Well, of course get angry, let it out—and then move on. But get the money you are owed for the work you do. Recognise your financial worth and don't accept less. Advocate for yourself—we'll cover this later in the book too—it takes courage. Read Carrie Gracie's book *Equal* to fully grasp what you are up against. Wise Up.

CHAPTER TWO

Self-Sabotage
And Other Stories We Tell Ourselves

With enough hurdles to jump over in the outside world, you would think that developing a habit of self-sabotage would only be for the crazy ones. Think again! Stopping ourselves from achieving what we want in life and business has become a serious malady. It now fills the screens and pockets of many an expert and coach.

As I mentioned in the last chapter, the three most over-the-top internal obstacles are to overthink, over-analyse and over-label. Women in particular have an extraordinary talent to over think, over-analyse and over-label what they do and say in life. It becomes an obsessive behaviour pattern without us even realising. From fussing over our appearance, the long apologetic introductions, the way we speak, what we write and more, we show how we question and label ourselves with every breath. It becomes an erroneous belief that sinks deep into the blood stream, cajoling the person into concluding that they are not good, smart, intelligent or capable enough.

It gets to the point where the stories we are telling ourselves have more relevance and influence on our success than any external obstacle could ever do to us. We can become so skilled at self-sabotage that it goes viral. It breeds doubt in others. It begs you to study your imperfections and errors in the same judgemental way. It starts another negative trait of 'comparison-itis' and then FOMO (that dreaded Fear Of Missing Out).

And it has reached epidemic proportions in many areas of the Western World. It has turned healthy inner reflection, constructive criticism and common sense into a laughing matter. In fact, common sense is just too simple to be taken seriously.

The idea that you must have therapy and a life coach is now part of our everyday vocabulary. Open up about a hiccup in your life—you need a consultant or a psychiatrist. It is the problem that is laid out, dissected a thousand ways (over a ten-year-period) and not the solution. It is the problem that is blown up into the trauma. If you are happy—you must be hiding something!

I have had at least two 'coaches' complain that I must be false if I am always appearing so happy. I have seen coaches demoralise a potential client in a workshop just to make her feel 'less' so she would sign up for more 'help'.

Let's face it, we all have encountered some trouble and strife in our life. And, perhaps in hindsight, we observe our own part in the mess. But then to have a coach rub their hands and say, "I got ya!" is truly a sign of our wicked times.

That is not to say we don't need support, accountability and solid advice. Humans have been turning to each other to release their problems and ease up the stress through sharing with another for thousands of years. The shoulder to cry on is truly a great comfort. A way to pause, process, relax and move on. Sometimes this is exactly what we need to have; an objective view of our stalemate, our obstacles, or the very thing that is holding us up.

I think it is important to explain from the beginning that we all have difficulties in our life, call it stress, strain and trauma. Yes, we need to air these and get our feelings out. But there's something else we need to do to remain healthy. . .

Michael Beckwith,[1] author and New Thought Minister puts it succinctly:

Number One: *"It is what it is–accept it."*

It doesn't matter what has happened in your life. Some of you have had bad things happen in your past, really disturbing things, they really messed your life up.

It is what it is, accept it. Either you are going to control it, or it's going to control you.

Number Two: *"Harvest the good."*

There's good in everything and the more you look for it, the more you'll find it.

Number Three: *"Forgive all the rest."*

Forgive means to let go of it completely. Abandon. Just let it go. Quit dwelling on what's wrong. Forgive all the rest.

One of my favourite quotes about forgiveness comes from Danielle LaPorte in her book *White Hot Truth*[2]: *"Forgive me but I am not ready to forgive."*

The point here is about learning to let go and heal your own past in your own time and at your own pace.

Fear in All Its Glory

For writers, authors, speakers, spoken word artists, story performers and entrepreneurs, fear can turn a good show into a mess. Our confidence drops to the floor, our courage is shamefully shy and no creative juices flow.

Fear is a non-touchable concept, an emotion, a concern, a state of panic and anxiety. And usually it is powered by our glorious imaginations.

If we make a list of all the things we fear, from spiders to bogeymen, flying to falling, failing in business to speaking in public, we will shock ourselves at how silly we sound. Fear is relative, right? It is how you perceive it and how you handle it. It's even a lot to do with who is with you at that moment, or doing it *to* you.

If we think about fear in terms of surviving in a war zone, refugee camp or nuclear fallout, fear becomes extremely real. Equally, if you are physically threatened or abused, your fear is rightly warning you of imminent danger. Often, though, our fears are of our own making.

I am not belittling anyone's experience of fear. I am asking you to reflect with a sharp eye and honest heart at the stuff you create in your head. I am referring to the story you tell yourself.

Many of us fear the loss of loved ones and the fear of illness. These are real and affect our lives deeply. But if they haven't happened why are we spending our time and energy on them?

Much fear comes from a lack of solutions to our situations or apparent problems. Fear develops from mistakes, from other people and from personal assumptions. Fear grows from judgements and unconscious bias. It's like a 'what if' virus that grows and makes you ill, or stops you from stepping up.

For many women, fear is more complicated than this.

External situations play into our internal mindset and vice versa and create a cocktail of fear. And fear in any combination, mustn't be shamed or dismissed.

One Dark Night

In 2012, I spent some time in San Francisco promoting my poetry book, *Words on the Wild Side.3* I stayed with friends outside the city in a residential area. I noticed there was a cinema close by and I told my hosts I would catch a movie that evening.

They said, "Don't walk, especially at night."

"Why?" I exclaimed. "It's only about a 20-minute stroll."

"We don't advise you to walk at night, especially by the station, it's not safe."

I decided to catch a matinee showing of the film and walked down in daylight to the cinema. I observed carefully, the side streets, the areas without lamp posts and timed my journey at 19 minutes.

The film finished around 7.00pm and yes, it was dark. So I briskly walked on the side of the pavement where there were more people. As I turned past the station, the people started to thin out. Soon I was alone. I had about ten more minutes to reach home.

I became alerted to every sound and rustle. My eyes were shifting from left to right. The trees suddenly became very noisy. I decided to cross the road and walk on the quiet street right in the middle.

As I stepped off the pavement, I jumped and let out a scream. I saw something. I was bristling with fear. I was terrified that a man in a hoodie with a knife was close to me and ready to strike. I stood in the middle of the road struck by fear and frozen to the ground.

It was only a few seconds, hardly a minute, when I realised I had actually jumped at my own shadow!

First, I was relieved, then I laughed—loud. I felt stupid, I felt safe, I felt ridiculous and I ran the rest of the way home.

I had feared the unknown, so much so that I had created in myself the very fear of my own shadow. Yes, it could have been dangerous, risky or unsafe. I don't deny that women especially are right to be on their guard. But nothing happened. I had pushed myself into a fearful state all on my own.

You Have Nothing to Fear, Darling—I'll Protect You
Unfortunately, for women and girls, some men do represent a real fear. It is not just in our heads, it is real. In a recent report, more than a third of girls have reported sexual harassment and fear for their safety.[4] Another report talks about the fear that girls have around boys and men.[1]

This is the point where internal and external obstacles

become confusing for many women. Doubts lead to low self-esteem and indecisiveness. Our 'fear' to travel and go out at night to see a speaker, hear a poet, or attend a theatre show is seriously hampered by a fear of being attacked, harassed or abused. It is in our heads because it is real. External obstacles are internalised, they become embedded in our psyche and this leads to overthinking, over-analysing and over-labelling.

Husbands, policemen, doctors, priests, fathers, brothers, uncles and legal guardians; these men are there to protect and cherish women. Or so the various books, guidelines and marriage laws state. But every woman knows that to 'love and obey till death do us part' is a heavily loaded phrase.

Girls and women know a different story, have a different experience. Men told us they would protect us but what they forgot to mention was all the other men that do not protect women and girls. Most abuse comes from the boys or men a woman or girl knows, is related to or has a relationship with.

Women's Aid UK conducted a report into femicide, defined as the murder of women because they are women. The report reveals how much women are protected by the men they know: the fathers, uncles, brothers, husbands, exes and boyfriends.

The latest Femicide Census report, published in

December 2018, reveals that 139 women were killed by men in 2017, and 40% of cases featured 'overkilling'. Overkilling is extreme violence, over-the-top, extra violence, often after the woman is dead. Three quarters (76%, 105) of women killed by men were killed by someone they knew; 30 women were killed by a stranger, of whom 21 were killed in a terrorist attack.[6]

It suggests (what many women already know either by instinct or experience) that it is the very men who are supposed to protect us that cause us the most fear.

It is not irrational, unreasonable or insane to have fears about standing at bus stops, train stations, walking home alone, or in any open space. Why do women and girls fear these environments? Because it is where men hang out, where they are free to roam, where they know we are not safe, because they have been telling us that. Because teachers, parents, social workers, police and judges tell us. Don't take sweets from strangers, don't do an endless list of things without the proper protection of a—man!

Whether we look at Rio in Brazil, Glasgow in the UK or Montreal in Canada, town planning and public transport do not consider the requirements of women. And who uses public transport most? Who are the people moved to high rise and isolated urbanisations? The most underpaid communities in the world—women.

In her book *Invisible Women,*[7] Caroline Criado Perez

has an infinite collection of information revealing the enormous gaps in data referring to women's lives. If an abusive or violent event happens outside of the house to a woman, girl or a group of females, and they are not accompanied by a male, or are wearing inappropriate clothes, or are inebriated, then they are the cause and reason for the violence or abuse.

The investigation and outcome depend far too much on questioning why and what was a woman doing out, dressed like that, in that condition, at that time of the night. **Not** the violent event.[8]

In the United States, 51.1% of female rape victims reported being raped by an intimate partner and 40.8% by an acquaintance.[9]

In the UK, according to Statistics from Rape Crisis England and Wales, approximately 90% of those who are raped know the perpetrator prior to the offence.[10]

It seems to highly contradict what men are telling us. The fact is that there is a very real problem for women and girls venturing out alone, on their own, or disobeying the 'rules'. Fear of being accosted, insulted, abused sexually and violently are real.

It is not a safe environment out there and it restricts, contains and prevents women from Stepping Up and Out.

But let me bring it back to the writers and speakers and highlight the following 'fears' that interfere with our progress. Mansplaining, bullying, intimidation, verbal abuse, and revenge porn. Online abuse. These are not irrational, preposterous or exaggerated 'fears'.

The very people who make the laws also perpetrate the crimes. No wonder it is so hard to be clearly heard, profoundly understood, or definitely believed if you are female.

Women do have a heightened instinct for survival. They are often more aware of threats and danger than many men, but at the same time the risks and hazards of external obstacles often breed obstacles of the internal kind.

It is important to remember that many men experience the same internalising of external problems. Not just amongst the LGBTQI+ but heterosexual men too. We learn fear from each other as well.

Fear is a complex topic, especially for women. It is the 'how do I keep myself safe and still go out and take part in life?' dilemma. And later in the book, we will look at courage and confidence, which are the best tools to handle our fears.

That Over-the-Top Thing

Christine Lagarde, former head of the International Monetary Fund, in conversation with Angela Merkel, the German chancellor, admitted that they both had the same habit of overthinking and over-analysing a speech or presentation, as mentioned in *The Confidence Code*[11] by Katty Kay & Claire Shipman. Many top sportswomen confess to this over-analysing habit too.

Studies show that men have a very different approach. For one, their voices are more likely to be heard, unconscious bias doesn't hold them back. Neither does a lack of confidence to speak off the cuff.

"The confidence gap (between women and men) is a chasm, stretching across professions, income levels and generations, showing up in many guises and in places where you least expect."
Kay & Shipman - *The Confidence Code*

The conclusion from Kay and Shipman in their detailed and supremely researched book is that even women in powerful occupations still over-analyse. Women double check, repeat and rehearse, study, over prepare—try to be practically perfect in every way. We fear being judged, over-looked, ignored, dismissed, not recognised or credited for our value, worth and knowledge. We fear rejection, being laughed at or belittled. The need, desire and struggle to be twice as good is rampant among women from all backgrounds, cultures and generations.

And it's not because we are neurotic, anxious women. Evidence of secrecy, lack of transparency and belittling are the tactics firmly in place in all powerful institutions. Women still have a hard time being recognised, valued and getting paid in the same way as comes naturally to rewarding men.

Unconscious bias is the term used but with resistance to change so persistent it feels more fitting to call it *'conscious'* bias. There are numerous examples when the bias is contrived and deliberate.

Fear of Success

One of the most extraordinary things we humans can do to ourselves is to fear success. We work so hard to achieve, to reach a certain status, position or pay result in life, but when a big opportunity arrives we back down. Fear of becoming famous or well-rewarded scares a lot of people, but once again women more than men.

Here is a list of the ten famous fears related to success:

1. Fear of too much work and being overwhelmed from it
2. Not living up to the expectations of others at the top
3. Not satisfying your clients/readers/audience
4. Fear of the big money
5. Fear of failing as soon as you begin
6. Fear of not looking the part

7. Fear of not coping because the attention and scrutiny is too much
8. Fear of not having a normal, quiet life
9. Fear of selling out
10. .Fear of becoming someone else

That is quite a list of destructive and disruptive behaviour going on! A crushing catalogue of self-sabotage. This is where self-belief and self-confidence knock on your door. You have to choose: Step Up & Stand Out or back down? And women often back down!

- Are you protesting?
- Are you saying: Not Me!
- Are you rebelling?

Then you are in good company. Haven't we got enough on our plates without adding on this self-destructive extra weight?

- Isn't it time to be Heard, Understood and Believed?
- Isn't it time to Step Up & Stand Out?
- Isn't it time to feel Confident, Courageous and Creative?

Yes, it is. Let's start now!

Some Tough Love
...Or as Mark Twain said:

> *"I am an old man and have known a great many troubles, but most of them never happened."*

Feedback is essential to improve. Take feedback from those who have your interest and your back, whom you respect and who respect you.

Here are three steps to start to dissolve, distinguish and dismantle any urge to self-sabotage:

Step 1. Admit your folly
Step 2. Decide to change
Step 3. Take action now

Sounds too simple?

Just because it's simple doesn't mean it's easy to do. Pushing for change comes with new learnings, new mistakes, action steps—then more learning and mistakes. Overnight success takes years.

All those irritating clichés about struggle making you stronger and hardship more grateful have some truths in them. Just don't fall into the punishment pit of the self-sabotage trap.

I remember going for a band audition. It was in a

studio in Willesden, North West London. Myself and seven men intended on getting the part. Three guys sat on the sofa, their horns (a friendly word for a brass instrument) between their legs. One guy kept his in a case and the other three stood around jesting with each other. It was 2am. My instrument stayed in the case and I observed the musicians greet and jest with each other until it was their turn to play.

Finally, I was called in, the last person at 3.30am. And the first thing the three men in the studio recording room said to me was: "How long have you been playing?"

Now, I ask you dear reader, what would have been the best answer at that time in the morning?

Dealing with external obstacles and internal ones at the same time is a real confidence killer. It affects your mental and physical health and wears you out.

It is time to acknowledge your obstacles and find a way to move on, clear the space and rise up!

Decide and act upon it.

Confidence and courage can be learned, and once accessed, you will see an immediate increase in creative energy. But first, it is necessary to kick out any obstacles, interferences and restrictions. Clear your decks and desks of any mental vandalism. Do not add more self-nuking stories to your life.

Remember those foolish hang-ups and take a walk on the light side of life.

As Elbert Hubbard, the American writer, publisher, artist, and philosopher says,

> *"Do not take life too seriously,*
> *you will never get out alive."*

Along with a little Tough Love, I encourage you to learn to laugh at your mistakes.

To laugh at your crazy self-sabotage ways. To laugh and let go.

Perhaps for some, it is understanding that it is all relative and life goes on. For others it could be a more logical approach and realising it is just another point of view—not everyone's. Then again, you might check over the criticisms or comments and find something useful, a spark of enlightenment, and make a relevant change to your work. My point being, there are many ways to handle fear and criticism and stop spinning down into the self-sabotage abyss. Each situation may need a different approach and some scrutiny is always needed.

Reach out for advice, guidance, even help. Sometimes it is just what we need, an objective eye, an experienced mentor or coach. Someone who can offer a view from the outside and put things into perspective for you.

In my own mentor work, I have seen how important it is for a person to off-load, transfer, let go, release, shift and relieve the worry by sharing and talking it out.

I would like to offer here some practical steps to encourage you to let go of your inhibitions, internal and internalised external difficulties/problems. I suggest practical action to help get you out of your head, shift up your funk, shake your low state of confidence. Because I believe it is the action that starts the germination.

Remember that many of our internal obstacles are rooted in inhibitions that stifle, repress and silence us. You can't blame yourself, you can take responsibility for your actions, but internalising the external problems is like feeding the weeds. Don't let it settle inside you.

As Michael Beckwith said, and I repeat:

> *"It is what it is—accept it.*
> *Harvest the good.*
> *Forgive all the rest."*

Practical Steps
If you write poems and you would really like to perform them, say them out loud, make videos of you speaking, and go on stage to deliver them, then you will have to Step Up and then Stand Out.

Here are five moves:

1. Rehearse your poems so much you can ditch reading them.
2. Edit as you go. Turn your written genius into Spoken word magic. Add the colloquial touch.
3. Video them. Go Live on IGTV, Facebook, your local community centre, library. Hell, if you are brave enough—go busk them.
4. Find like-minded poets. Listen to them perform. Learn from them. Go see the Big Stars live and on YouTube.
5. Write more. Keep inventing new poems, pieces, lyrics. Keep writing, performing and learning.

For authors and bloggers wanting to have a wider reach, greater recognition and financial rewards, I offer these five moves:

1. Time to come out! Go public. There's no way around it nowadays. For your written work to soar, you need a public face, image and profile. Social media offers enormous possibilities for new connections of the widest range in race, gender and the famous. It is also low cost.
2. Accepted number one? Then, next move. Work out your public image, your brand colours, clothes and backgrounds. Whatever you want to try,

whatever you have dreamed of or imagined—try it. Even on a smaller scale, you will gain huge knowledge, wisdom and experience.

3. Ask for help and guidance. Watch what others do, no comparing or copying—just learning.

4. Look into paying for PR. One day you will need it—so start gaining experience now. You can hire a PR consultant to teach you how to pitch, email or verbal. And, you can hire a PR team to work with you.

5. Start blogging. Set up a web page—keep it simple but let the world know you exist. Google is watching and advertising you.

For speakers and story performers, the moves are similar to the first group. Here are my five moves:

1. Learn and rehearse, polish the words, get your stage presence and personality out there. People will remember your words but also your face, energy and digital links.

2. Reach out to other performers on all platforms, video, stage and page. Do your research. Watch, listen and learn from those in the public eye.

3. Get help, hire a coach, or pay an expert to build your skills and profile. Invest in yourself.

4. Make, create and find opportunities. Start with making videos. Learn from them: your voice, tone, volume and expression. How are your vocal dynamics? What about body language? The light and shade? Practice these skills.

5. Repeat all the above again and again. Become professional in your approach. Do some free gigs, be generous because you are confident.

And business women and entrepreneurs will benefit from all the above too. In fact, these 15 moves are relevant to writers, speakers and business people across the board. Visibility is essential and by practising these steps, you will gain immense confidence and feel heaps of courage and see your creativity unleashed.

I have included above many practical steps to start to overcome the restrictions that external and internal (and the combination of both) have over us. In the chapters that follow there will be more about the action steps you can take. This is just the beginning.

CHAPTER THREE

Courage

A New Definition of Courage

Too often when we use the word courage, we picture a fireman, policeman, or superhero. Yes, I know we now call them firefighters and police officers but the images are often masculine.

Courage and bravery are so intertwined with physical acts of strength and rescue that we seldom give the space to recognise other forms of so-called fearlessness. Of course, it is all relative. I have no yearning to go cave diving or parachuting, it holds no interest or desire for me. In fact, there are numerous activities I would never undertake, but that does not mean I am not brave or courageous.

Many of the physical acts are for adventure, to stimulate the adrenal glands. However, there are numerous acts of charity carried out by teams of women, unpaid and uncredited, from working with disadvantaged children, to older and infirm adults. All of these are acts of bravery, but somehow are seldom recognised in the same way.

Is it because heroism is considered a physical act performed by the physically strong?

Is it because gallantry conjures up men on horseback?

Is it perhaps because we still associate bravery with daring, valour and spunk?

And how many of these acts still invoke masculine images in our minds?

If we move away from physical actions and displays of courage and bravery and think about:

- Speaking in public
- Asking for a pay rise
- Talking about pay
- Asking for more
- Requesting less hours or tasks for more money
- Asking for a divorce
- Questioning your rights
- Saying yes
- Saying no

. . . And a million other social and personal asks and questions. Do we consider these brave actions?

- Is bringing up two children under the age of ten and working part-time a brave position?
- Is moving to another country at the age of 60 a brave act?
- Is quitting a well-paid job in corporate to start a small business a brave move?
- Is standing on stage telling your personal story brave?

It's all relative I hear you say. And of course, it is. But seldom do we recognise and credit these actions or consider them as signs of endurance, grit, tenacity, guts, boldness or enterprise.

And part of the answer is because the definition of courage and bravery still solicits a male image of prowess.

What image comes to mind when you read or hear the word Heroine (often misspelled as heroin!)? Do you picture a globetrotting, mercenary, opportunist swashbuckling person?

Besides Wonder Woman and a few noble Queens, see how many heroines you can name (outside of family and friends)!

The Courageous Saboteur

There is also some tricky self-sabotage involved in expressing courage, because as women we so often feel obliged to fit in. We believe it is our duty and obligation to follow society's rules, the social and moral codes—very often to the detriment of our real abilities, talents and genius. We tell ourselves those 'keep it small' stories. And the world tells us to play it safe too—we're not trusted if we stand out.

We are educated and guided to believe that we must keep silent and invisible, as much as possible. There are boundaries and limits challenging many people in this life, but no more so than for women and girls.

Caroline Perez Criado, in the preface of her latest book, *Invisible Women*,[1] writes, "Research has revealed that. . . most of recorded human history is one big data gap. . . the lives of men have been taken to represent those of humans overall." She continues: "When it comes to the lives of the other half of humanity, there is often nothing but silence."

And she further remarks that our 'culture is riddled with these silences. In film, news, literature, science, city planning, economics—everywhere and in everything.'

Doing courageous acts and actions for a woman is like skating on thin ice, backwards and wearing red high heels!

Never mind the courageous saboteur, you also have Big Brother watching you!

It is real, sometimes subtle, sometimes blatant,

and often just plain old unconscious bias. The male perspective has been accepted as the human perspective. For many women and girls with talent and genius this comes across as a limiting way of expression.

It is a tyranny of repression. Punishment guaranteed. From ostracism to fines, imprisonment, medical butchery and/or neglect.

But I digress into the world under the Glass Ceiling. Yes, it takes courage to Step Up & Stand Out in this world full of 'unconscious bias'.

There will be obstacles, both in the outside world and inside our heads, as you've already read. There will be detours and hurdles. But, at some point, you will have to decide and take an action. Don't get caught in that trap! Be proud of yourself for your brave decisions, but don't let that be the end. Do the brave action too.

Remember that every step of the way is a courageous step. Every little move you make towards your goal, passion and ambition has worth and value, and is a sure bright sign of courage. Even if you get knocked back.

Just because the world doesn't recognise your bravery, doesn't mean it has no meaning, significance or value. But you have to see and believe in your calibre, excellence and quality. You must be aware of your assets, riches and wealth. These are the essential ingredients to showing courage where and when you need it.

Rebels and Other Disobedient Women

Know your strong points; the things you excel at and love to do. Become clear and aware of your special talents and skills—this starts the courage-pot boiling. Equally, knowing what you can't do, don't do and shouldn't do are vital to your courageous thermometer rising.

Write a list. Two columns. In one, write down what you like doing and in the other, what you don't. Check through them once more and then dilute to your top five skills and top five 'never again' efforts. For most of us, the things we most enjoy are the things we are best at, and equally, the things we hate doing are not our strengths! Make sure you include everything, all the little skills you may be taking for granted. You can touch type? Write it down, as not everyone can. You take great photos? You are nifty with design? You are empathetic? Write all these abilities down on that list.

This is an extremely courageous step: admitting what you can do and can't do. It's not written in stone. You can grow and expand your knowledge at any time. Every time you learn something new, the list will adjust. But keep on acknowledging your little courageous steps as you make them.

Knowing who you are and what you are good at is about being real with yourself. Not putting yourself down, or into a category or box that says, 'useless'. Whether you are a writer, speaker, story performer, spoken word artist or entrepreneur, having a courageous attitude is essential.

It means taking courageous steps.

Offering to take the lead, the responsibility and the first steps.

It will require you to speak up and stand out.

To put your hand up, to lean in and shout out.

Sometimes you will have to gang up, call in the team, nudge and encourage others. If the world's not on your side, create a world that is. Find your people.

There will be days when you feel the energy of courage and others when you don't. That's life, don't beat yourself up.

I have walked off a stage, after performing my poetry in a spoken word club, feeling like a lump. Like a complete embarrassed failure. I felt they hated me, didn't hear or listen to me. Ignored me and talked over me. All I thought about was my failings.

I didn't give myself credit for getting up on that stage and performing three of my best pieces. Now that took courage. How it came across was only my interpretation of the audience's response; it wasn't necessarily true!

We are too quick to judge and assume. We imagine and conjure up what others 'could be thinking'. We put words into their mouths before they have said a word or even noticed us. And we become obsessed with getting the 'likes', applause, credit and praise.

Here is a list of some courageous women, including writers, artists, political leaders, a NASA astronaut and mathematician, that some of you may not know.

- Isabel Allende
- Cheri Honkala
- Rhea Seddon
- Judy Chicago
- Shirley Chisholm
- Dr Dorothy Height
- Audre Lorde
- Mary Jackson
- You
- Me

Acts of Courage to Recognise
- Writing your story, your version or opinion—and publishing it.
- Writing your experience and speaking about it or publishing it.
- Speaking about all of the above topics on stage or video or TV, in a webinar, on radio or a podcast.
- Writing your story and/or experience and performing it on stage.

- Starting an online Biz Niz with services to sell.
- Staring an online Biz Niz with products to sell.
- Doing any or all of the above and add on. . .
  doing it with children, parents to care for and
  a day job. That is, doing all of the above and
  performing the Three Little Cs.

It is time to re-define what is courage is for you. Start
another list of the courageous actions you took last week,
month, year or ten years ago. Remember all the little
brave steps you took. Don't judge or compare. Re-define
courage for yourself.

Being courageous is also about rocking the boat,
questioning everything, breaking rules that don't serve.

Being a rebel **with** a cause.

Some Powerful Re-Definitions of Courage

In the writing and speaking business (that includes
spoken word artists, story performers, journalists,
bloggers and their copywriters), opportunities to Step
Up & Stand Out are everywhere. There seems to be stages
and videos on every platform—all accompanied by some
form of text—the written word is everywhere. We still love
reading!

So it is about paying attention to all opportunities
and asking yourself honestly and without prejudice:

- Could I do this?
- Would it benefit me?
- What tools do I need?
- What tools have I got?
- What are the financial rewards?
- What are the financial costs?
- Will it overwhelm or burn me out?

You can ask yourself these questions in any order and as many of them as you feel fits the offer on the table.

Don't overthink, over-analyse or over-label anything.

Repeat this sentence out loud every day.
Turn to your team players and accountability partners for advice and support. It is really important to find mentors, coaches or accountability partners who are honest with you, and give you constructive and relevant feedback. You do not need people to say you are brilliant just to please you. The right team, support or coach will provide the nudge and encouragement you need.

The rest is yours. You are not bungee jumping, cave diving or tightrope walking. Please don't go down that comparison road.

If the option or opportunity is there and you would love to do it, then Do It. Clear the clutter and do it. Feel excited and scared; that will give you the energy to Step Up and then feel the fear and Stand Out!

Whatever happens, remember you took that step, you gave it your best, performed authentically and even secretly loved it! That is courage. That is pure courage.

Film it in your mind and play it over and over.

Write it down and read it—again and again.

And if you videoed it –watch it repeatedly and be proud of your achievement.

Give yourself some tender, tough-love commentary.

But don't take it personally.

Be professional not perfect.

Courage comes in so many shapes and sizes. Reclaim yours.

CHAPTER FOUR

Confidence

Every Which Way it Works for You

What image comes to mind when you think of a confident person?

Is it composure, a look of authority, a decisive style, the ability to look people in the eye? Is it about charm and charisma or even money? Do we associate a confident person with intelligence, or having a professional manner or even a particular way of dressing? And, are we born with it? Do you conjure up a woman or a man when you first think of a confident person?

I think that confidence is taking any action you want to take without being held back. I believe we are all born with confidence but then life happens. Our parents, society, teachers and other adults start to influence and train us, and there begins the obstacles, setbacks and other misfortunes that slow us down or take away our natural ability to be confident human beings.

So, for most of us, clearing away the clutter, damage and extra baggage is the first step to resuscitating our confidence.

Or as Pat Evrard said about being a confident person:

"You are either one, or on your way to become one." [1]

Confidence is contagious and so we are drawn to what we believe to be a confident person. In theory, that means if you stand in front of a mirror and practise a confident 'look'—the mannerisms, poise and body language—you could transform into the part. Could it really be that simple? I think that if you:

1. Want, need and have the desire to be confident (again!)
2. Are ready to make decisions on your options, choices and opportunities
3. Are open to change and taking action

. . .Then you are already in the realm of brilliant, confident thinking. You just need to start taking action. Here's how.

To En-courage or Not to Encourage
Encouragement is key for the development of children,

students and anyone learning something new. It is a fine blend of enthusiasm, feedback and recommendations for improvements. It is a combination of giving and receiving attention. In fact, receiving and giving attention to and from parents, teachers and professionals is a normal and healthy form of developing relationships.

If we grow up in an environment where there is a lack of encouragement, feedback and reciprocal attention, it can be all too easy to digress and give up. If your teacher is calling you lazy or lacking in some ability, or your parents call you stupid, then you start to believe it could be true. We are easily fed and led.

Most of us have heard statements from either our parents or a teacher or so-called friends like these:

- "You're dumb."
- "You will never be anything."
- "You're no good."
- "Don't waste your time on that you have no talent."
- "Girls don't do that."
- "Boys don't do that."

I am sure we could all write a long list of these discouraging phrases.

If the act of encouragement is essential to the

development of our confidence, how can we bring more of it into our lives?

One way is to dish it out generously. Rather like smiling, once you start to encourage others, it starts to reflect back. It is about viewing your cup as half full, focusing on solutions rather than problems, and seeing outside of your box and comfort zone.

Sometimes we hold back from encouraging others because we are resentful of their success or feel like failures ourselves. So we don't want to help others. It may sound petty, but it's human. Become aware of where your lack of encouragement may have originated. Those gaps of attention that gave way to insecurities, doubts or even fears. Pinpoint them, but here's the thing—don't over-analyse, overthink or over-label them (remember those killer inner obstacles from Chapter Two!). No blame or regrets. No shame or hatred—a good session of cursing or banging on a few cushions never hurt anyone and could actually serve as a great release!

And believe that when you begin to encourage others, you are developing super leadership skills too! Now doesn't that boost your confidence?

Paying Attention is Not Multitasking
They say that women have a talent for multitasking. Feeding the baby, while typing an email, and speaking

on the phone. But in my mind that is because she has no one else to help. In many cases this kind of multitasking leads to small mistakes, whether it is a spelling mistake in the email, or giving the wrong number while speaking on the phone, or spilling the baby's milk on her shirt. Yes, women should be applauded for coping in difficult circumstances when they multitask, but that doesn't mean it's the best way to do things. When women are over-stretched with the Three Little Cs—cooking, cleaning and caring—they are distracted.

When it comes to giving and receiving attention this is quite another skill and involves no multitasking of any kind. Paying attention when someone is speaking to you, especially one-to-one, is a fine quality. You are listening with both ears open and your one mouth closed. You are not thinking up a response or fiddling with your phone. Paying full attention to the person in front of you shows respect, intelligence and confidence. Why? Because learning to pay attention and to listen respectfully shows your confidence. You are not rushing to reply, you are not forming an opinion or an answer in your head—you have the confidence in yourself to sit back and take it all in—confidently.

It is the difference between listening to respond and listening to understand.

This can be done on a grand scale. If you are on a

panel for a book launch or conference, featuring on a webinar or video, sharing a stage with other speakers, being interviewed on radio or TV. In numerous situations you can show that your attitude is both professional and confident by displaying an ability to pay attention.

You Can't Please All the People All of the Time

For me, the first step to developing confidence was to become aware of the negativity, of all the useless, non-productive statements that were thrown at me growing up. That meant breaking a few rules, which fortunately came naturally to me. The way children continuously ask 'why?' was a habit I never lost. And it is a habit I encourage others to continue.

Asking questions is not encouraged in many societies. It is considered everything from being impertinent and rude, to immodest, improper and insulting. Ask too many questions or challenge too many rules and you are suspected of being an anarchist or a philistine. Even as I write this, I feel an urge to ask why are so many 'things' in life considered to be unquestionable?

Is it to protect those that make the rules? To keep us in the dark and behaving well?

If the rules in your life do not serve you then it is most definitely time to question them. After all, as many famous people have said and sung, *"You can't please all the people all of the time."*

When do we grow out of questioning and asking 'why?' Is it when we get bored of the answers. . . or lack of them? Is it when we start seeking our own answers? Or perhaps when we are told enough times not to ask any more?

I was frequently told to explain what I meant by 'why?' which really confused me, until I came to the conclusion that it was an adult way to shut me up.

Asking questions may not always provide you with the answers you want, but those kinds of answers sure give you a clue as to what you are up against.

As a teenager at school during a History lesson I asked, "Why are we studying all these wars? Why can't we investigate the lives of the queens or what women did when men went off fighting?"

My teacher (a man) couldn't answer and found a quick way to write me off with, "It's not relevant to our lesson today!"

But I kept these questions alive in my head. "So, when men went off hunting what did women do? Why don't we know? And why are there so few women scientists or leaders?"

I asked a lot of teachers and always got brushed off or told "not to ask silly questions!" No wonder my school report stated: *'Georgia is a good student but she can't concentrate.'*

My point being, you can never satisfy all the people, and questioning will make no difference, so you might as well start questioning and asking anything and everything that doesn't sit right, feel appropriate, or lie within your values and limits.

Reminders:
- Questioning doesn't have to be aggressive, but it can have an assertive edge.
- It is worth checking your facts and data if you are going to argue your point.
- Gang up/team up with fellow colleagues, it builds confidence too!

Now we have dealt with people-pleasing, one of those barriers to confidence, it's time to go back to basics. What is confidence? For me it is all about Self-Belief, Attitude and Personality.

How to Create a Bucketful of Self-Belief
What have you learnt in your life?

Start by writing out the first thing that comes to your mind, even if later you want to scratch it out or find it ridiculous. Sometimes that is the best starting point;

the funny and the ridiculous. It may also include the things you learnt that no longer serve you—but they all have their value and place in your life too.

Include in that list everything from riding a bike to baking a cake.

Include all the dance routines, games, football, tennis or marble games you ever played.

Make that list hefty and lengthy.

Don't be tempted to think about what you didn't do, learn or achieve.

Keep focused on the list of everything you have ever learnt.

Isn't it looking impressive?

Now you have the foundation and you are shutting out the stories that say you can't do this or that. It is time to focus on what you have and how to build on it.

So, ditch the overthinking, labelling and analysing business. Forget the self-depreciation talk—it might be popular in comedy but not for real-life. Time also to dismiss, disown and dismantle all of these negative tendencies and start to move forward.

Some people need to forgive, some to forget, while others have to let go—and others still—all three. Whether you let go or spend time in therapy, before you do, remember you cannot change the past. You can only change the way you remember or review it. Ignore the unimportant, and move on.

Don't be afraid to say you are good. Time for you to blow your trumpet, do a little self-praise, big yourself up! It is just another way to advertise and self-promote; a key part of any business or profession.

Shift your focus onto what you have got, have achieved and accomplished. For writers, speakers, authors, spoken word artists, story performers, female entrepreneurs—our stories and experiences are often the core of our message. We have our lives on paper and on video and stage. We need to be solid about sharing it.

Being vulnerable is hugely fashionable and a great asset on some platforms, but make sure you don't let your emotions overpower your intelligence, your professional attitude, or performance.

"Be the heroine of your life not the victim."
Nora Ephron - journalist, filmmaker and writer

You Need Attitude to Reach Altitude
Your attitude is often what people notice first, so they say. From your body language to facial gestures and choice of words, we all make our first impressions. Are we respectful and polite, do we smile enough, speak at the right volume and chose the best vocabulary at the

right speed and tone? These are the indices we pick up when we meet someone new.

So, how is your attitude? How do you come across to others? What feedback do you get? Jokes aside, find out what are the genuine statements others say about you.

There is a difference between 'having an attitude' and 'having a positive attitude'. The latter gives you power over your circumstances. When you take on a positive attitude towards yourself and your life everything changes. It is like having a professional attitude towards you and your work.

It is the difference between saying:
- "I can't do this, I'm out."

And:
- "I don't know much about this yet but I am ready to learn."

Admitting you don't know something is a fine quality to own. But make sure you follow it up with the learning. Develop a taste for knowledge, become inquisitive as to how things work, what things mean—and always double check your source of information. Remember to question everything.

Admitting and asking will show you so many new

ways to express yourself and establish experience. This is also a great way to boost your self-belief.

She's Got Personality

I am sure you can think of a few people that you are attracted to because of their personality. It could be family, friends, an author or actor that you admire. Then think about the characteristics that stand out for you that you respect and perhaps want to emulate. The qualities and values that a person shows, shines and shares.

As writers, speakers and business people we read and watch others as part of our learning and education, to stimulate and inspire us. We watch videos of our most interesting and insightful speakers. We read books and articles from authors we appreciate. And often we research and follow them on social media to discover more about what makes them tick. To discover their personality and what we have in common with them. From their words—written or spoken—and their appearances on video or stage, we deduce more about them and start to form our opinions.

Now it is time for you to write that list of all the beautiful characteristics that make up your personality. Think about your qualities and values, the things you respect and honour. Then, collect together the compliments you receive that others appreciate in you.

That will be quite a list, I can assure you.

Your personality is your Unique Attracting Point, your U.A.P. It is what makes you 'you', and sets you apart from the other seven billion people on the planet.

As Oscar Wilde famously said:

"Be yourself. Everyone else is already taken."

And this is what creates attention from others. All these amazing characteristics you possess are the features and traits that your audience, readers and clients are drawn to. Once again, don't overthink it, analyse it or label it.

When I was writing and producing plays, I had many struggles and setbacks but I filled seats and heard applause too. The feedback was mixed because you can't please all the people all of the time. Even the negative comments I could use to go forward. But I remembered the encouragement and the compliments. Things such as how much they admired my humour, passion and tenacity.

My personality shone through my work and that is key in your speaking, writing and client work. It is about creating a personable energy. So let it come out. Smile with your eyes, use more body language and pay loads of attention with your ears.

Confidence comes with self-belief, attitude and

personality. And it can be learnt. Every day you hone into self-belief, attitude and personality, your confidence will grow.

Your attitude towards others defines your level of confidence. And be prepared to receive attention too. It works both ways. When someone pays attention to you, compliments your work, or asks you to Step Up & Stand Out on their radio interview or to be the keynote speaker—be ready to receive.

Don't stop to overthink, over-analyse or over-label it. Don't hesitate or shy away, back down or doubt yourself. Be ready to receive the attention and Step Up to the part of a confident, speaker, writer, story performer or entrepreneur. Attitude is about receiving too.

As you build your self-belief and attitude, your personality starts to glow. You will begin to express your character, magnetism and charisma.

Confidence comes when we stop comparing ourselves to others and send out encouragement instead. It comes when we realise that we are never going to please everyone, so we may as well get on with doing things our way. And it is built from self-belief, attitude and personality. Every day you step into these magic three, your confidence will grow.

CHAPTER FIVE

Creativity

The Rules From Schools

We are all born with imagination and creative abilities, and we develop them through learning and practise. What opportunities we have to receive education and training is another thing altogether. But we all have some creative abilities in our blood, our soul or heart, call it what you like.

Unfortunately, our access to literacy, schooling and study depends far too much on location, class, gender and race.

Can you imagine that still today, many girls have no educational opportunities? According to UNICEF, there are 32 million girls of primary school age not receiving any kind of education.[1] Somalia, Niger, Liberia, Mali, Burkina Faso, Guinea and Pakistan continue to restrict education for female children.[2]

Even for those who can access education, the

curriculum for most schools around the world leaves little scope for imagination! We are taught subjects riddled with sexist, racist and out of date information. I know that I was so bored and distracted during History class because it was all about senseless battles, kings beheading women who didn't obey or produce boys, taxing the poor and an extraordinary taste for debauchery, excess and waste.

Yes, much has changed, especially in higher education, but still, whether you are studying the arts, politics or science, you wouldn't believe there were any females, or people of other nations in the world, who contributed in any way at all.

Then to confound things further as Bob Proctor states in his book, *It's Not About The Money*[3]:

"We're taught from our earliest days in school to conform rather than be creative."

I call it the Rules from Schools and I wrote about it in *The Rule Breaker's Guide*.

All that pure, creative, natural genius suffocated and drowned out by narrow-minded teaching and limited curriculum. The emphasis on fitting in and sticking to traditional roles is damaging to the human creative spirit.

We are dissuaded from our true talent and told to leap on the Con Belt of life (the Conveyer Belt), and just go round and round. What if we had more diverse teachers, or brave parents and an abundance of role models from across the gender spectrum including different nationalities? What if we balanced out the enormous data gap in history, science and the arts, and trusted children to come up with their own arguments?

I believe children's natural abilities could flourish. "Alas and Alack," as some male character in Shakespeare said. So much natural talent squashed so early.

Bob Proctor continues:

> *"We have to raise our hand in order to speak,*
> *colour inside the lines and walk in line.*
> *We are taught to search for the 'right' answer*
> *rather than offer creative solutions."*

Of course, no one is suggesting anarchy. And neither is this about teacher hating. It is about allowing questions to be asked and checking the source of the rules and regulations. Developing a healthy inquisitive mind and encouraging creativity. It is about bridging gender and race gaps. It is about taking the edge off competition and more on collaboration and team.

I recollect my childhood desires to sing and dance on stage, I dreamed of writing music and plays and working with many talented people. Then I was told:

- "You aren't the right shape or height."
- "How will you make a living?"
- "That path leads to trouble and drugs."
- "You haven't got enough. . ."

As it turned out, some twenty years later, even after the teachers, education curriculum, family and friends said I couldn't do it—I did go on to do all of those things, off my own initiative.

So no matter if they say it's not for you—you will never succeed and the rest of it—go and re-discover those dreams and passions. Revive and revise them. See if they still inspire you. It's never too late to re-discover what you once loved. You are never too young, or different, or anything else to rekindle that passion within you.

Maybe you can't run in the Olympics or become a leading soprano, but you could coach, do sports massage, or become a musical director. You could be involved in some area you never imagined before, more suitable and appropriate to your talents and experiences of today. And even if your creativity doesn't turn into paid work, it will light a fire in you that will bring energy to your life.

For writers and speakers, our creative and imaginative abilities are at the core of our work. We are often discouraged at an early age to not follow a certain creative path. We then may believe that we lost out, we didn't obtain enough knowledge or education on the subject we felt inspired by. And then we get all the negative feedback that it's too late and you can't make a living or support a family as a creative person.

For all of us in the written and spoken world, this kind of negative 'talk' are the Rules from Schools we need to dismantle and disown.

Where to Buy Some Creative Vitamins

How often do you go to the theatre? Perhaps attend a show or a live band or music concert? Do you visit museums or exhibitions? Do you go to listen to speakers, spoken word artists or even story performers speak their words? When was the last time you went to take part in a live sporting event? And I'm talking with real people here, not sitting and viewing YouTube, Netflix or any other screen-based entertainment.

You will be surprised to know how many of the above 'live' activities can stimulate the parts of our brain that stir up more creative juices.

I call them the Vitamins of Life. Whether going to a basketball or tennis match, a horse race or dance show, a concert or an exhibition of new tech or organic foods—it all depends on your openness to learn and gain more knowledge. And all of these events will invigorate your brain, heart, soul and pen!

It is important as writers and speakers to feed our imagination and creative sources.

It is part of our personal education to learn more and receive new ideas and incentives to express ourselves. You may find that attending a concert will relax you, and take your mind off any frustrations or anxieties. Going out dancing will exercise your body as well as your mind and leave you happy and exhausted. Watching a live sports event will stimulate your determination muscles and fill you with resolve and adrenalin.

It is important to set aside time every day to play! Now this could be doing 30 minutes of yoga, watching a comedy show, taking a walk, making biscuits, dancing to your favourite song or even having a nap. It is time set aside for you—time investing in you.

There is an interesting relationship between creativity and pressure. Some people have that lightbulb moment when they are relaxed and others will have a surge of creativity or genius when they are under pressure—such as a deadline situation.

All of these activities and more are the vitamins you need to accelerate your creative energy.

What's Creativity Got to Do with Me?
So, how does creativity fit into confidence and courage, I hear you whisper? For a start, and let's be clear, being

creative is trying out new ideas, fresh thinking, finding solutions and being inventive.

Having a creative spirit is about self-expression, delving into our instincts and our intuition.

Being creative is about acknowledging our uniqueness and valuing our work. When we create, we remove inhibitions and obstacles, and we touch down with our 'authentic' selves.

Being creative gives us confidence to explore and express, and urges us to take action—and that is courage.

Being creative is tapping into that child-like state of not caring what anyone thinks—it is all about play.

I remember when I was about 8 or 9 years old, playing in the garden of my mother's house. I was making sandwiches from the leaves of a lilac tree and sticky earth. I selected green and evenly-shaped and sized leaves, collected a handful of earth and added some water, stirred to a nice sticky consistency. Then, I began to put the dark, 'peanut butter' earth between the lilac leaves and lay them out on a branch, beautifully decorated with a petal from another flower. They were exquisite in appearance and. . . totally inedible. I was creating—that's all that mattered at that moment.

Believe me, writers and speakers, creators of the spoken and written word, we need to be, feel and exist as creatives. It is our place of genius where all our brilliance flows.

Where our best ideas are born, nursed and rehearsed. Where we edit, trim and design. Here lie the seeds of future changes, happenings and events.

Once you light your creative fire and keep it alight with regular vitamin intake, it's about moving your creativity from your safe space onto video, stage or page. Preferably all of them.

Difference is Your Superpower

How many times have you heard, 'you can't reinvent the wheel', 'nothing is original', 'everything is a copy'?

Not much imagination there. And it's true, wandering off the straight and narrow isn't without its consequences, and in some cases, punishments. Standing out from the crowd with your printed word or spoken word gives off a strong independent statement.

I recollect some of the most successful people who at first, or for a long time, didn't fit in, from Rosa Parks, Malala Yousafzai and Gabourey Sidibe to Nelson Mandela, Oskar Schindler and Mahatma Gandhi.

They all stood up for their values and principles. They did not conform or follow the herd, they moved in their own direction to make a change.

They expressed their individuality, uniqueness and creativity. And they did it with confidence and courage. They wrote and spoke about the injustices affecting them stepping out of their safe space and using their difference to make their point.

Don't hide your gifts or shy away from your talents.

Don't resist being your bold and beautiful self, there are no benefits at all on that path.

Your difference is your superpower if you encompass it and be authentic with it. Be yourself.

Every time you give the best of yourself you perform authentically.

Slamming Words

Albert Einstein said,"*Creativity is intelligence having fun.*"

And having fun, and laughing, are certainly important contributions to the creative process. But it is also about solving problems, thinking up new ideas and alternative versions. It is what is known as insights, epiphanies or lightbulb moments, you know, that feeling of "Eureka!".

Maya Angelou said, *"You can't use up creativity. The more you use, the more you have."*

Creativity is not just about music or art, it involves natural intelligence, the aptitude to express your expertise, your craft—your genius in your own special, original way. And words are the form of delivery we use most. Verbal or written, expressed with passion, drama, colour, sound or music, or any other creative twist you might come up with.

Be creative with your language, be inventive, love your thesaurus, look at other languages—yes, discover new words. Listen into conversations on the bus, train and a queue in a shop. Don't get involved, but listen to street talk, chats between friends and lovers. Watch a couple of soaps on TV, a comedy show or an excited sports caster. You don't have to do it for too long, just picking up snippets is the idea. Listen out for new phrases and vocabulary.

Watch the facial expressions, the raising of eyebrows, twitching of the nose or curling lips. Be aware how people use their hands and shoulders when they speak. Become observant to body language. They all offer great things to write about or emulate in your own speaking and performance.

As a creative person, being observant and paying attention are your attributes and your tools.

So, my friends of the written and spoken word, we know how creativity gets squashed out of us from an early age. We are aware of the education system and the Con Belt lifestyle causing narrow thinking and a 'cup is half empty' mentality. It is important to leap over those hurdles whichever way you can. Because your difference is your superpower. It's your uniqueness, your special creative energy and it needs to be out there.

From the written and spoken word, changes have

happened, worlds have rocked, and differences have been made. Think of all the books that have impressed and altered your way of thinking and your lifestyle. Or the speeches that stirred the world (not the political or racist propaganda, although it illustrates the point).

Nowadays, we have so many excellent outlets for our written and spoken words. Feelings and emotions are expressed through words. Words on the page, stage or video. Words that we can use to fill others with reason, value and worth. After all, that's why we do it, to connect and communicate.

I offer two of my favourite spoken word artists, bringing to the forefront some real history (or herstory): Hollie McNish poem—'War's Whores'[4] and Gil Scott-Heron—'The Revolution Will Not Be Televised'.[5]

Creativity, Courage & Confidence
On the days when I doubt my abilities, in other words when my confidence is low, I find I need to tap into either my courage source or my creativity bucket.

When I feel low in the self-belief department arena, I tap into some creative activity. It could be anything from giving water to a plant, reading an article, another chapter in a book, listening to a song I love. For you, it could be watching a film, seeing a play, listening to a spoken word poet or TED Talk.

Or I might find it is actually a spoonful more of courage that I need. More courage to finish that chapter or blog post. More courage to rehearse that poem or speech again. More courage to do another video or reach out to a new contact. And every time I take another spoonful of courage, my confidence rises. The more I accomplish and achieve the more confident I feel.

When I feel confident and courageous, I know creativity will be by my side too. These beautiful Three Cs work with each other to make you stronger.

"Creativity takes courage."
Henri Matisse - artist

Writers and speakers, lovers of the written and spoken word and entrepreneurs, it is your time to Step Up & Stand Out.

And whenever you feel one of your levels of creativity, courage or confidence ebb, know you need to call on the others to support you, to lead you back to that confident, courageous and creative state of mind, heart and action.

Now it's time to get to work!

CHAPTER SIX

Now That We Have Found Our Genius What Are We Going to Do with It?

We have boosted our confidence, our courageous muscles and creative energy. Now what are we going to do with it all?

This chapter is about how we can put it all to work. How we bring more opportunities, promote ourselves, build our reputation and profile, and receive our rightful rewards.

As we build our professional profile through learning, repetition, experience and hard work, the Three Big Cs will flourish and our kudos improve. The importance of being and remaining consistently visible is vital in this fast, fickle world of today. Online and offline, the competition is grand and the attention span of many users is about 8 seconds. Our work is cut out. . . and you can do it!

How to Become a Famous Writer

"Writing is show-biz for shy people."
Lee Child - author

Once upon a time, authors were considered as shy, quiet people. They rejoiced at the publication of their books; the lucky ones who had agents, publishers and well-connected friends in high places. Occasionally, they read an excerpt from their book at a launch party and signed copies if they were already famous. But most authors had no public profile.

Then self-publishing arrived—big time—it was 1979![1]

It opened the door to print on demand (POD) and the digital printing world exploded. You could print 10 copies or a thousand. It was a digital tech revolution. For five centuries there was only one kind of book available— the printed book—courtesy of Johannes Gutenberg, the first European to use movable type and build a printing press. Now we have e-books too. And it meant that everybody had access to showing and sharing their written genius.

Of course, the tech revolution has moved on at the speed of—a tech revolution—wickedly fast. By 2018 there were over a million self-published books for sale.[2]

The trends in the year 2019 according to online publishing company IngramSpark were:

- Political and social satire.
- Poetry is popular; creativity is entrepreneurial.
- Short books rule OK.

Now that is a very broad spectrum. The doors are open and creativity is at the top of the list.

However, authors today are now under pressure to promote their own work. Giving a 5 or 10-minute reading from your book is no longer enough. Writers need a public face.

In one way it has become easier. All you have to do is get on to social media, have a plan, a strategy, a team and some persistent hard work. It is that simple. Your reader, the buyer of your book, the person who writes the review and spreads the good news regarding your work, needs to know more about you.

- They want to know about you.
- They want to see your face.
- They want to know what else you have written.
- Where you have spoken?
- What do you do when not writing?
- Who influences you?
- Whom do you admire and respect?
- Whom do you recommend?
- They want to see you on IG and Twitter.

Your visibility is required on as many platforms as possible.

Here is a list of low cost self-promotional ideas for writers and authors:

- Start a blog.
- Build a website.
- Write an eBook.
- Hunt for reviews.
- Acquire testimonials.
- Turn your Facebook page into a community and offer challenges with your book as a prize.
- Create videos for YouTube and on your website with excerpts from the book.
- Start vlogging.
- Follow other authors and engage on their social media pages.
- Network offline.
- Attend events and conferences for learning and networking.
- Build that brand of yours.

Begin with the option you prefer the most and start to build. Take your time, don't fall into overwhelm territory. It takes time and persistence. You will need to be consistent in your content too. And resistant to comments and empty criticisms. And you will also need to be insistent on being yourself.

All of these shakes and moves are possible with some dedication, positive vibes and hard work.

You must have noticed I have mentioned the phrase hard work three times. And it is true, some of it will feel strange, like you are way out of your comfort zone and as though it is difficult. And these are the times when you will call on your team for support and reassurance, when you will conjure up your resistance and use your determination to push through the lows and downs of your rise to fame.

The Vibrant Life of a Speaker and Spoken Word Artist
All of us verbal artists start with some form of written work, whether it is doodling on a serviette or tapping on a typewriter or keyboard. The written word is the seed we plant that later turns into the magic of the colloquial form. From the little notes, scraps of paper, recordings on our phone or lengthy documents on our word processor, we deliver the gold and treasures of our art.

At a conference I attended recently, I met up with a publisher who spent his time asking the speakers if they had a book. He praised their speech, asked to see their website and know more about their next event. But what he wanted to know was had they written a book.

A book would be the long version of your speech, your story, or the collection of your poems and prose. A book would open doors into another market. A book is your business card and your product.

In 2019, 2.2 million books were published. Reading has not gone out of fashion. In fact, in a survey in the United States in 2011, 81% said they believed they had a book in them.[3]

Writing a blog, article or a book is cool. So turn those notes and scraps into blogs and articles and even a book.

Now you may have already branched out on to video. It is one of the most popular forms of entertainment and learning. However, so is having a book. With YouTube and Facebook dominating the video scene and the ease of creating videos on your phone, video is popular, but remember that many people read the text / the subtitles on a video—so writing is back and right on the screen.

Be prepared to turn your spoken word magic into the written form too.

A Hard Day's Work

As I mentioned above, hard persistent work is essential to building your profile, your following and the sales of your services and products. Let's first define 'hard work' for writers, speakers and entrepreneurs.

Dedication is key; it means putting in the hours. And it includes commitment, which means sticking to it, even when it feels hard or you feel demoralised. Discipline and determination are central.

And then, hard work is love and passion for what you do. It is being open and flexible but with that 'never giving up' energy. Hard work is persistence and sometimes it is just going for it. Hard work will feel harder on some days and on others superbly rewarding.

Hard work is what will make you succeed. Always keep in mind you are accumulating 'word miles', experience of life, people and business. Sometimes the rewards for hard work aren't obvious, but don't be dispirited, because, again, overnight success takes years.

Authors know that although the writing process can be enjoyable, putting together a book is hard work and dedication. They also know the editing, proof reading, and to and fro with publishers is hard work.

Speakers and spoken word artists know that repetition and rehearsal is central to their performance. This is dedication and determination at play. And business women and men know that persistency and consistency will deliver results. They know exactly how much work is involved in building a business up from scratch.

That is all it is. It is about having that professional attitude—whatever happens. Turning a mistake into learning and experience. Showing up regardless. When the lights go up—it's showtime—it's your time.

When it comes to hard work, keep your focus on what you want to achieve. Develop a healthy self-care routine. Delegate and team up.

What's Your Favourite Colour?

Knowing how to promote yourself, showing off your best side, and having a consistent practice, helps your audience identify and pick you out of the masses.

Your PR team, business strategist, PA or VA and business coach will show you how to create an unforgettable image. Of course, you can also go down the DIY route and use your own creative abilities. Observing others, learning from your role models. But there is nothing like investing in yourself. And more about that later.

Meanwhile, collect your favourite quotes, sayings and books that you have read. Name the people who have influenced you and perhaps changed something in your life.

Remember the people who trained you and the accountability they gave you. Think back to all those who encouraged you in one way or another.

Pay attention to coincidences, blessings, lucky breaks and pure magic you have experienced and received.

These people are your followers, admirers and perhaps collaborators.

From all these interactions you now have an idea of what you can do to prepare yourself for video, stage or page.

It is time to create your brand, your appearance and your colours for your website, your videos, radio interviews, TV or stage appearances. The fonts and images you will use. The way you will appear to your readers and audience.

So what are your favourite colours? What suits you? What really compliments you? What is fashionable that accentuates your eyes? Seriously, you need to be aware of these details. Even if you show up for a radio interview and you think no one will see you. Think again, as you never know who else is in the studio, who you will meet at the desk when you enter or who will be exiting as you go into the studio—and the ever-in-demand-selfies.

"Look like a million dollars and you will get a million dollars."
Georgia Varjas - *The Rule Breaker's Guide*

Find your style, freshen it up from time to time and enjoy it. You can, of course, hire a brand strategist, brand coach or stylist. Google has the list to start with. Go by recommendations or observations you have discovered from other websites. Don't be bullied into using colours and fonts that do not resonate with you. Branding is a lucrative business.

There is also branding and life coaching. The two have merged together in many areas of the writing, speaking and entrepreneurial world, both on and off line.

A coach specialising in brand will be looking to create a personal brand for you. That means your web, blogs and social media 'look' is consistent throughout. Your photos, videos and show-reels all have the 'You' flavour.

According to Jeff Bezos, founder of Amazon,

"Your brand is what people say about you when you are not in the room."

Everything you do and say tastes, smells and sounds like—you! And that means people will remember you.

Women at Work—I Wanna Break Free

"Women-owned businesses are the fastest growing segment of new business start-ups, and black women's businesses are a larger share of black-owned businesses than white women's businesses are of all white firms"[4]

"While aggregated data is often challenging to find, the

recent Global Entrepreneurship Monitor (GEM) found 126 million women starting or running businesses, and 98 million operating established (over three and a half years) businesses. That's 224 million women impacting the global economy—and this survey counts only 67 of the 188 countries recognised by the World Bank."[5]

And much of this is led by gender inequality. [6]

It's exciting news that female entrepreneurs are on the rise! Women have had enough of social and financial constraints and they are breaking free. Jumping off the Con Belt of work.

They are the new mothers, leaving corporate or other professions to take time off to parent and cherish their new born and toddlers. They are women in their twenties who found no career options from their time at school and have decided to 'do something completely different'. They are women who have left university with a degree in accounting (or whatever) and really feel totally disheartened by prospects, pay and conditions, and would rather do something entirely different than become an assistant in a bank (or whatever!).

They are women 35 to 40-plus saying enough is enough, I am going solo! They are experienced women 50-plus using their many years of work and life experience to start a business.

And they are inventing and creating extraordinary opportunities for themselves and other women too. They are designing anything and everything from clothes for breast feeding mothers to coaching and business strategy. Women really are the mothers of invention!

This includes female spoken word artists and story performers. Women making a career from speaking on video and stage. Whether you come from a corporate background, showbiz, or even the university of life, opportunities for women to spread their wings and create a business they love, which gives value and provides financial rewards, are all possible.

If you think you are too shy, then you will need to call on courage to pick you up to take that plunge and speak from the podium or front of stage when you launch your book or do any promo for it. Practise will make you proud. You will push through.

If you think you are not good enough, then you will need to call on confidence.

Check out the list of accomplishments you wrote. Do a little self-care, remind yourself how talented you are. Remember all the events, articles, speeches, poems, stories, services, products you made happen. Remember all the people you touched, encouraged, learnt from and shared with special, amazing and inspirational benefits.

If you think you have nothing special to offer or you

cannot think of what to say—or if you have that Blank Page Syndrome—you will need a dose of creativity. Change up your routine. Attend a concert, art show, exhibition, museum, sports event, theatre, dance. Go be inspired by other talented artists. Discover and learn.

Yes, it is a roller coaster ride, a free-falling experience, zip-lining at times. It is also a great adventure in exploring, observing, paying attention, thinking out of the box, re-invention and wisdom. Subjects you don't learn at school.

It is also about turning your focus away from self-depreciation. As we said in Chapter Two, it's about harvesting the good. Use what you have and make the most of it. Feel proud of your achievements and learn how to dip into confidence, courage and creativity lessons when you need them.

Your genius is all yours—go out and use it—enjoy it and benefit from it.

CHAPTER SEVEN

Standing Out in a Crowded World

*"Fitting in is a short-term strategy,
standing out pays off in the long-run."*
Seth Godin - author and former dotcom business
executive

There is fear, mystery and a heap of old legends surrounding the idea of Standing Out. There is also stigma and resistance to show your personality and passion. There is this shame about showing off and blowing your own trumpet.

Well, in the online and offline world of writers, speakers, spoken word artists, story performers and entrepreneurs, this attitude is a load of destructive rubbish.

You have to promote yourself. You need to Stand Out. It is important that you know and recognise your skills and sell them. It is vital that all your essential ingredients show and shine when you appear on video, stage and page. You have to find your way to 'big yourself up'.

It is interesting to note the negative implications around the phrase, 'showing off'. It suggests it is a deliberate action to get attention! Isn't that what you do in business? Create an impact to acquire attention? Do something with your work, written or spoken, to gain the attention of your client, your audience and reader? How can you run a successful business without attention? Or, to put it another way, how can you help the people you want to help if you don't have their attention?

Business coaches are constantly advising us to be more visible and to offer enticements to our services/ products. If that isn't showing off our values and content, then what is?

In order for us to stand out in the crowd we need to be wearing red, or pink, or whatever colour you prefer. The premise is that you stand out and that means selling yourself, authentically with passion, personality and performance. It means you do not apologise for being who you are. You are loud and proud.

It is crucial that you find a way to promote your work because if you stay at home and hide, your work will not be seen, recommended or paid for. It requires you to leap, jump, hassle and hustle right out of your comfort zone. It implies you will get in front of the camera, create videos, write that book or blog, and stand on stage and perform.

If the phrase 'showing off' makes you curdle, see it as sublime self-promotion. Regard it as a personal revelation of your charisma. Witness it as a disclosure of your fascinating personality. Time to uncover, unmask and bring to light your finest features, metaphorically and practically speaking, of course.

You want to spread your message, your opinion, your excellent service and valuable product? Time to rise and shine and advertise like hell! Let's remember one important fact. We all sell something. Everything we do in life is about selling.

You sell to your children the benefits of eating spinach or going to bed early or doing homework. As teenagers we sell to each other our skills on video and phone, our ability to bungee jump and skateboard. At work we sell to our bosses our professional expertise, our savvy, dexterity, competence, experience, deftness, proficiency, technique, artistry, command, ingenuity, knack and aptitude. We sell every time we start a new relationship; our greatest and kindest attributes. Human beings sell to each other.

For those who are resisting the word 'sell' because your parents, religion or other influences told you it is a dirty word, and a greedy objective, then substitute it for:

advertise, market, boost, trade, contract, exchange or move.

Life is about business and business is about selling, sales and rewards. But you don't need an intricate business strategy. You need to be strong enough to be yourself and be visible.

Confidence, courage and creativity are the building blocks for standing out. Without confidence, you won't get out there. Without courage, you won't say what you truly believe. And without creativity you won't have anything interesting to share. So get nurturing those Three Big Cs and you'll find yourself standing out before you know it.

Passion—Personality—Performance

> *"Passion is energy. Feel the power that comes from focusing on what excites you."*
> Oprah Winfrey - actress, presenter, producer

Passion is energy—high and positive. However, the Oxford English Dictionary sees passion as: 'Strong and barely controllable emotion'!

If you believe that description, you may turn inward, feel guilty about expressing passion, or even label yourself as shy. You may even have been taught that passion suggests sexual desire and therefore has to be controlled. There are numerous hidden and subtext rules around passion. From moral, religious and suggested ways of behaviours—passion is a loaded word.

I have been accused of being too passionate. My energy, emotion, expression, fire, tactile style and volume of voice and gestures were considered unladylike, too emotional, out of control, and hysterical. All of them insulting and reeking of *The Taming of the Shrew* scenario.

When a woman behaves passionately, it is often seen as a sexual expression. Somehow loud, crude, even vulgar. Even a suggestion of alcohol or medication use can be implied.

When men are passionate, they are commended as showing spirit and leadership qualities. We may be aroused by it but it is not frowned upon in the same way as it is for women. Men are never 'asking for it'.

When I am enthusiastic I am passionate and when I feel empowered I feel passion. When my confidence, courage and creativity come together I really feel passionate.

- What are you passionate about?
- What are your top five passions in life?
- Do you have hobbies, activities or sports that you are passionate about?

Make a list of topics, subjects and hobbies you are passionate about.

Having and showing your passion in your writing, in your speech, and in your performance can only add to your connection with your audience and readers.

It is as in music and dance, the ability to express equal amounts of passion and technique into your work to bring it to life. The idea is to show contrast, dynamics and moments of excitement.

Passion is a powerful communication tool. Discover it, rehearse it and let your audience know you have passion for what you do. But equally, if you are not feeling passion for your work—then you need to examine honestly why and what you are doing. Is it time to reinvent yourself?

And use this energy in your work. Allow your passion to become your purpose because one day it will become your profession. For example, I didn't think in the beginning that writing poetry would lead me to writing books or stepping on stage and performing my work. My passion became my profession.

Personality Sells Your Magic

"We should take care not to make our intellect our God, it has powerful muscles but no personality."
Albert Einstein—physicist

Your personality is an integral part of who you are and how you show up. Your energy, your aura and charisma, and your character traits. Personality is also a big part of Standing Out. Time to gather up your finest characteristics and set them free.

While doing my research for this book I asked Google for a definition of personality. It offered the 3 types of personality, then there were the 8 personality types, and then I saw one for 16 different personality types. I am sure in every psychology book, manual and bible there will be more 'types' divulged. But we know that your personality is what makes you uniquely you and that is the feature that you need to bring out when you Step Up & Stand Out on video, stage and page. It is about you recognising the best sides of your character. And, if it is not apparent to you, find a way to bring it out and reconnect with you.

Time to make a list—a long one—of all your super personality traits. Personality includes your charisma. No, you can't buy it and yes, you can develop it. Charisma is your allure, magnetism, appeal, even your dazzle and your pizzazz.

First check out who you believe has charisma? Is it a celebrity, a family member or a speaker you saw on YouTube? Study their selling points, what makes you like them? What makes you watch the whole video? And what makes you want to have some of that charismatic personality?

Pick out the top three to five charismatic traits you admire. Pin it down. Is it a quirk, a peculiarity or a trick? Is it an attractive, assertive or decisive style? Is it perhaps about self-confidence, vulnerability or humour?

Hone it down to a few words, now check your own list and see where the two meet—your own personality traits and those of your charismatic role model. Then, you can create your own unique brand of charisma.

Remember there is quiet and calm energy as well as fiery and exuberant energy. There is a time and place for both. On video and stage your personality sets the vibe. Your audience has come to watch and view you, not just because of your amazing content, but because you have passion in your body and a message, which is revealed through your personality. This can be a quiet steely strength that takes people's breath away, or a loud, impassioned roar. But it will be you shining through your own way.

Time, again, to pick out your favourite role models from the dance, music, sports, and art worlds. Study their personalities and see how many mannerisms, idiosyncrasies and qualities you have in common.

Think about how your favourite personality traits show themselves to the world. How do you look and act? For example, maybe you show your confidence with the Buddha smile. It is the one that stays on your face after a big smile. It is the one that lifts your cheek bones, feels peaceful and doesn't show teeth. It is the smile that shows in your eyes. And it is a super smile to have when receiving compliments, listening to a conversation, being asked a question, and before you start a live video or live talk.

Other traits of your personality can include your laugh, the way your eyebrows move when you are interested. Or, perhaps silent gestures of nodding, touching a hand or shoulder? Become familiar with these and they will be a natural part of your branding as you network and meet new people in your work.

Performance

The word 'performance' has had some bad press. Most dictionary definitions go down the performance management systems route and are about ranking and evaluation. According to The Business Dictionary it is:

'The accomplishment of a given task measured against pre-set known standards of accuracy, completeness, cost, and speed. In a contract, performance is deemed to be the fulfilment of an obligation, in a manner that releases the performer from all liabilities under the contract.'[1]

Some have described it as an act which implies

something staged or false. I wrote a lot about performance in *The Rule Breaker's Guide*, and I want to repeat a key point here:

"Every time you give the best of yourself you perform authentically."

To me, performance is simply believing in yourself enough, and respecting your audience enough, to give it your best. In the written and spoken world it is important to not get caught up in the sub-divisions of this word. When you get up in the morning and start to prepare for an interview with the BBC to promote your book, share your opinion or speak on your top subject—you are preparing for your 'performance of a lifetime'.

There is confusion between presentation and performance; one is professional and business-like, the latter is theatrical and orchestrated. But there are similarities.

Whether you present or perform you will have some preparation, rehearsal or practice involved. If you are professional you will perform your presentation and you will present your performance. Rehearsing does not make what you perform inauthentic. Rather, it brings it to life, just like a writer edits their work, or a sculptor chips away at their marble. Rehearsal gives your audience, whether in a meeting, theatre, book launch or business conference, the opportunity to see the best of what you have to offer.

Wikipedia offers this explanation:

'Performance is completion of a task with application of knowledge, skills and abilities.'

So, let's not waste time on bickering over the meaning and let's start adding some attitude, personality and verve into your performance.

Opportunities, Options and Choices

"In the middle of every difficulty lies opportunity."
Albert Einstein - physicist

There is an abundance of quotes about opportunities that imply you have to make them yourself or, like a sunset, you will miss them. Then again, they are like buses and another one will appear very soon. Opportunities are lost and forgotten but also found when you least expect them. Create them and take them. Anything is possible with opportunities.

Start by writing out all the options and choices you

have on your radar right now. As you begin to think about what is in front of you, more will be revealed. Persist with the list, it will surprise you!

I have had to search for opportunities on numerous occasions as a musician. Life before mobiles and Internet meant you really had to be inventive, step out of your comfort zone and take opportunities by the horns (sic).

I would go out to watch bands playing at clubs, when live music was popular. First, to see if I liked the music and could add some sax sounds to it. I was truly in command at this stage, deciding whether I could enhance the music with my melodic sax sounds.

Then after the gig, I would approach the band. Basically, I pitched to them. Many times, I was laughed at, insulted and told 'no' straight out. But I persisted, I was cheeky and insistent until finally I was given an opportunity to play with them.

Nowadays, for writers and speakers, there are more swinging doors than ever. Yes, it is crowded and competitive, but it has always been, it was just less obvious.

When you read autobiographies from people you admire who have reached great success, they often started from humble beginnings such as Oprah Winfrey or Bob Proctor. With their determination and 'never-give-up' spirit, they created and found opportunities that led to progress, achievements and success.

And we are back to those obstacles: glass ceilings, bamboo floors and casting couches, but now you know about them and you can make smart decisions, whichever way you turn. You have confidence, courage and creativity to pull out of your pocket to guide and advice you.

How to Be Red When Everyone Else is Pink
Online, offline, party or interview, how can you stand out and be recognised, create a stir and be red when everyone is pink?

Now, you understand how to be confident about your talents and skills. Courageous to act upon them. And with an abundance of creativity to keep going, you are ready to stand out.

Here are eight steps to stand out:

1. Walk tall and carry the posture of a dancer. It's all about your body language and people read it.
2. Dress to impress but wear what is comfortable. No point struggling in tight shoes or wearing a tie you fiddle with all the time. Be you at your best.
3. Listen—2 ears, 1 mouth. Don't rush to reply. Let your confidence shine by being secure enough to let others speak.
4. Hands up and lean in. Express your opinion and

point of view. What you have to say is as valid as anyone else's opinion.

5. Feedback—offer and receive it with dignity, respect and openness. As has been said before, encourage others and harvest the good.

6. Be generous and kind. It's not always about you, so compliment, praise and encourage others.

7. Be enthusiastic, passionate and professional. Always give your best, do the work, rehearse, practise—give your best.

8. Don't hesitate to say you are good, an expert or an authority on your topics.

CHAPTER EIGHT

Conquering the Demons

In this chapter I want to focus on how to keep the Three Big Cs—Confidence, Courage and Creativity—at our side, in our pockets, and close to our hearts and minds. How can we turn to each one when the other is not present or strong? And how can we vanquish the demons?Let's face it, we all have trials and tribulations in our life. Each one of us has emotions and feelings. We are affected by weather; too hot, cold or windy. We are stirred by disappointments and financial insecurities. The world is an unstable and uncertain place and all these external obstacles do sway, swing and swerve us. How can we deal with these pitfalls, those down times and waves of bad news?

As we have seen in Chapters 1 and 2, most of us encounter a variety of difficulties, both internal and external, so now let's get into how we can work with and defeat them.

How to Keep Going When the Curveballs Fly

First of all, let's be clear—having confidence, courage and creativity is not about magic, conjuring tricks or witchcraft. It is about building confidence in your talents, showing courage by using them, and being creative about making your way in the world—especially when the going gets tough. Rejection, criticism and lack of recognition, money and community, are enough to get you ducking and hiding, but they are common flying curveballs.

I know how disheartening it is when book sales do not flourish, as I expected mine to. When sales for my extraordinary once-in-a-lifetime event didn't sell out and when only one person showed up for my value-packed online course. I know what rejection, failure and let down is. But here I am. And the motto, meme and attitude I want to share is—never give up.

Does it sound easy to write? It isn't. There have been many days of hair-pulling and cursing in three languages. And sometimes, that is the best way to get that frustration out of your system. Of course, don't beat yourself up, or your loved ones, but find your way to release the tension, whether it is a walk and talk in the park or dancing the night away.

I have to emphasise the importance of self-care. I believe in taking responsibility for your own health through awareness and attention. If you need an hour off, a weekend away, a massage, a spa day with the Girls—make it happen.

Don't side-line your health, there is no way you can work, fulfil your dreams, passions and goals if you are sick in a bed. And if you're in the writing or performance business, then your work relies on you having that unique personality and getting out there. Physical, mental and spiritual wellbeing is essential for a nourishing and flourishing life—so start to look after *Numero Uno*.

Sometimes you have to step back before you can step up. Time away from your work (and I don't mean performing the Three Little Cs for yourself or someone else) can be both remedy and inspiration. However, don't spend that time wallowing in overthinking, over-analysing or over-labelling.

Curveballs come in all shapes and sizes. Having good health makes you fit to hit those balls away from you. Let's look into the detail of that.

Look back on your list of accomplishments and achievements with sharpened awareness. Get your foundations steady. It is paramount to keep a positive attitude in troublesome times. Rather than focus on what you don't have, take the time to look at how far you've come. Look back at the positive feedback you've had, the ways you have grown as a writer, performer or speaker.

Recognising and appreciating your achievements, skills and talents will revive your level of confidence.

Next step is to appraise the damage. What is happening or what happened? Did you lose business, an opportunity to speak, or do a TEDx Talk? What really happened? Assess the damage, evaluate carefully and ask yourself, what are the facts? How much have you actually lost? It might feel like the end of the world but it isn't. . . no one cares as much as you do!

Consult with like-minded and wise colleagues. Listen to their opinions and points of view. But always keep in mind it is just that—their opinions. You don't have to agree with them and you are your own boss—trust yourself first.

Start to prepare your revival. Discuss and decide alongside your top team and delegates. Create your Plan B and C. How can you harvest the good and turn it to your advantage?

Plot and act on the moves you need to solve and smooth out the problems you are facing. Take action. Focus on the solutions.

The Power of Your Team and Other Good Friends
Most times it helps when you can see the difficult situation from the outside with an objective eye. It could be looking at it from another angle or visualising

the bigger picture. The idea is to step back, release the upset, anger or frustration and have a larger image of the whole. Time for teamwork. Bring in your confidantes and collaborators. People who get you and share your passion. They also respect you for who you are and have your back. And if you haven't found them, then you are well overdue the acquisition of your team. Step out of your comfort bed, sofa or zone, and team up. Reach out to people you are drawn to—in this digital age your team can be global.

For writers it is about having a writing mentor, an accountability partner or fellow writer with whom you can confide and share your doubts and dilemmas.

Check out where your writing comrades hang out. And also look out for editors, proof-readers and copy writers, even ghost writers. You all share the love of words. That is enough to start a connection.

Speakers, story performers and spoken word artists need to go out and listen to live speakers. Network with the audience, stay to meet the performers, take time to hustle and bustle. It's time to let your personality shine, to connect, engage and share your hesitations and misgivings.

Business people know the value of networking, they know where their clients hang out. They know the art of paying attention and asking questions that prompt interest and curiosity. Build your networks to attract people who you trust.

Maybe you will need to turn to an expert or coach to improve, up your game or get over a pitfall. Somebody you can share your problems with, who will give you objective guidance and advice, and action steps to take.

Ask questions—question everything. Use your wisdom and experience to decide if this is the best way for you to go. You are not obliged or duty bound to follow their advice. Be open and keep your own counsel. Use your common sense to evaluate the people round you so you can move forward and deflect the curveballs.

The Power of Yes and No

Some of us find saying 'no' difficult and some of us find the word 'yes' just as tricky, mainly because these two short and powerful words often need attention and consideration before they are uttered. They are two words that can make or break a friendship, relationship or business deal. They are the words that can change lives for better or worse. They are the oldest and most powerful words in any language that can re-direct the course of history.

Ask yourself, are you quick to say yes or no? Do you always say yes or do you generally say no?

Perhaps you say one and then some time later go back

and change your mind and say the opposite. Sometimes after consideration, consultation and asking questions we change our minds. But do you resist or hesitate using either of them?

> *"When you say 'Yes' to others, make sure you are not saying 'No' to yourself."*
> Paulo Coelho - author

Sharpen your awareness when you say yes to a new project, client or coach, that it is really what you want to do.

> *"Half of the troubles of this life can be traced to saying yes too quickly and not saying no soon enough."*
> Josh Billings - humour writer

Are you saying yes or no to opportunities? Are you holding back to overthink, over-analyse or over-label? Are you letting your fear prevent you from answering? Fear of failure? Fear of being seen as a fool, or worse?

> *"If someone offers you an amazing opportunity and you are not sure you can do it, say yes. Then learn how to do it later."*
> Richard Branson - entrepreneur, business leader

Having a clear understanding of the meanings and outcomes of your yes or no response is for your own clarity. It is about taking responsibility for your answers and results.

If you need to take some time to consider your response, then take it—but don't let fear and overthinking make the decision for you.

Learn to say "no" to whatever harms or hinders you and "yes" to whatever serves or suits you. Develop your personal power by using these two words wisely.

Opportunities: Chance—Choice—Change

This title says it all. Turn your chance into choice and your choices into change to bring about the best opportunities for you.

Let's break it down. As Richard Branson says, chances are opportunities that you say yes to even if your mind is saying you are not ready or prepared. . . because you can learn as you go. This is an interesting approach and one that many men take. Women too often hesitate and go down the overthinking road and then miss the opportunity completely. Sometimes, you just have to go with your gut instincts and say yes and then learn on the way. If the person offering the opportunity believes in you, then it is worth taking it.

Naturally, you have to ask about pay and conditions

and timelines. Learn to tune into and trust your instincts and follow up with great questions.

You always have a choice. Sometimes, that makes it harder to decide and that wavering can lead us into the overthinking territory. For me, it is about seeing options as bright choices and positive possibilities. Some scrutiny is needed, maybe research, or an investigation into the company, the people or the location. All these things can make or break the opportunity, but also makes you wiser and richer for the experience.

Check out how you could improve the offer on the table, what you want to add or subtract, perhaps you should make a counter offer? Be confident about your contribution and value.

I did this when playing music for a theatre group. They wanted some background noises and sound effects and I suggested a melody to enhance a mood and a 4-bar section of atmospheric music in another part of the play. The director loved the idea. My contribution created an ambience, which was appreciated and financially rewarded too.

Be open to choices and invent them. Be creative as you now know how. Grab your courage, feel confident you can contribute and go for it. Make them an offer they can't refuse!

You have to love change! Change brings new horizons,

adventures, connections—opportunities. Be open and keep your boundaries. This might sound contradictory but there is great wisdom in recognising that life is full of paradoxes.

Your openness to chance, choice and change doesn't mean saying yes to everything or whatever is thrown at you. No, not at all. But it is about being observant, broadminded, receptive, versatile, resilient and ready. Ready to listen, question and decide.

During our rollercoaster ride to achievement and success, there will be glass ceilings and hurdles to face. We have our talents and skills. We have our experience and wisdom. And we have confidence, courage and creativity to turn to.

Now it is about tapping into any of the three as we need them. Recognising what is 'missing' from the act of the day or the decision we have to make. What and why we need that extra boost of confidence, courage or creativity. And turning to the lists we have made, the positive testimonials, the coaches, and colleagues we trust and know. It is about asking pertinent questions and creating opportunities and change.

Starve the fears and feed your desires, your ambitions.

Now is your time to Step Up & Stand Out.

CHAPTER NINE

Putting It All Together

Time to fly. Lights, camera and action. Time for you to get cracking, follow through and rise up on your platforms of video, stage and page.

This combination is electric and eclectic. To build your reputation, kudos and receive the rewards, it is time to Step Up & Stand Out on them. Are you ready? Or are you still holding back? Have you started but still need encouragement? Have you tried and not succeeded? Are you wondering when the good times will roll because you have been working so hard?

I have summed up the numerous roadblocks that you can encounter, including the ones we create ourselves and build upon. I have mentioned in detail how we can become overwhelmed from overthinking, analysing and labelling. We know the pitfalls of FOMO and 'comparison-itis'. We can recognise that downward, slippery road to the abyss of self-depreciation and self-destructive behaviour. We understand how anxiety and doubt can lead to a walk in the windy wilderness. We know how hard it can be.

But we also know how to dismiss and dismantle them by learning from our mistakes, by understanding how we contribute to the error of our ways and therefore have a say in the matter. We know how to vanquish the demons, to handle the hecklers of life, the critics and sumo wrestlers who wish us negative damage. We know we can call on the Three Big Cs. of Confidence, Courage and Creativity. Most of all we know we have it in us.

The Paradoxes of Wisdom

"Life gives you surprises and surprises give you life."
Ruben Blades - singer, songwriter, actor, musician, activist and politician

Life is indeed full of surprises, especially if you are quick to pick them up and prepared to take them on. Say yes to opportunities, create them yourself, team up, find and work with amazing collaborators. And all this enlightening learning and discovery encourages more smart thinking.

Challenges are everywhere and life is full of contradictions. This means that we need to do some wise thinking, reasoning and sharp evaluations on our beliefs and thought processes. To question with clarity the cultural boundaries we have built. To take responsibility for our health, life and Biz Niz relationships.

"Wisdom is paradoxical," says Danielle LaPorte in her book *White Hot Truth.*[1] And she is 100% right.

Thinking is one of our most under-used and under-estimated natural gifts. Unfortunately, 'thinking' is not encouraged enough at school and in society in general. Thinking for yourself is not on any examination board or curriculum. Many of us are so put off after 10 to 15 years of schooling, by an education system that promotes learning off-by-heart, copying, paraphrasing and being brainwashed.

Thinking for yourself, learning and reading what you want to learn, is usually only studied at the University of Life. However, when you start to discover, explore, observe and recognise more; your wisdom expands, your experiences grow and your knowledge increases. This is when you realise how many extraordinary paradoxes there out there in this world.

The following are inspired by Danielle LaPorte and relevant for artists, writers and performers.

1. Love yourself always *and* love the world too. Time to Step Up & Stand Out and be more

      magnanimous, more generous to all you encounter.

2. Forgive *and* never forget. Remember Michael Beckwith. Accept it. Harvest the good and forgive all the rest.

3. Show understanding *and* don't take any BS.

4. Open your heart *and* keep your boundaries, clear and strong.

5. Be realistic *and* idealistic. Be practical *and* make time to dream.

6. Be passionate, follow your instincts *and* keep your head clear. Lead with both.

7. Hold on to your beliefs *and* make many exceptions.

We are solopreneurs, we are creatives, writers and speakers, performers of the spoken word—and we are all in this together. We are extraordinary and somehow ordinary and that makes us unique. We are vulnerable and strong and we can be powerful with our written and spoken vocabulary.

By accessing our confidence, courage and creative talents and skills, we have the tools to follow through, level up, gain reputation and kudos. We know how to make an impact on whichever platform we need. We now have the right attitude and professional mind space to perform on video, stage and page.

We are clearly heard, profoundly understood and most certainly believed. And we know how to do this through our written and spoken formats.

Georgia's Gems

I want to leave you with a collection of little gems you can pull out of your pocket when the doubts, demons and setbacks strike. Some practical steps and mind set practices to encourage you to continue and never give up.

Having a great team around is about being understood, respected and recognised. Start the way you want to go on. If being understood is important to you, state it, ask for it and pay attention to it, both giving and receiving.

Do less of the Three Little Cs and more of the Three Big Cs. This is vital for women, mothers, men who are fathers and everyone looking after children, the ill and elderly. Balance, delegation and hiring a service to assist are your options. Take them, make them work for you. This is deeply connected to self-care and self-worth.

Asking expands your creativity. Feed it. Go and be entertained by other artists and vibrant people. And question everything. Adjust the rules that do not benefit you.

If you still feel uncomfortable about being happy with your work, or you believe it should be hard and long suffering to become successful, it's time to get out of that pessimistic, contrary and gloomy state of mind. Free yourself from mental slavery as the wise Bob Marley sang. You have the right to feel happy and fulfilled doing work you enjoy.

Money is not evil, poverty is. Learn to value your talents and worth. Ask for that money, tell them you want a pay rise and you want to be paid in currency not potatoes, free dinners or other perks. These are extras, don't mix up real money with favours. Get used to sticking your hand out on pay day.

You cannot do it all on your own. Delegate essential tasks that drain your energy. Seek out trusted mentors or coaches for feedback. Build a Mistress Mind circle or group to chew over any dilemmas. If you want to join a gang of rebel artists and learn to fly your way, seek out my coaching programmes through my website.[2]

In the end, being professional is a state of mind worth adapting in everything you do. You don't have to be a workaholic, a perfectionist, or an overachiever. Every time you give the best of yourself you perform authentically. You show up and give your best.

This is not a magic formula. Reading this book will not bring you fame or fortune—YOU will. All the guidance, coaching and assistance will not make you an overnight star. Only taking action on your decisions will. If you follow the steps you will gain confidence, courage and creativity. It is an exciting, thrilling and unpredictable pathway. Turn your learning into success. Use your experiences to build amazing teams and friends. And be open to all the incredible opportunities awaiting you.

The stage and your audience await you—*Rule It!*

Bibliography and References

Chapter One

[1] https://www.scarymommy.com/working-women-cartoon/

[2] https://www.youtube.com/watch?v=o9ZSKE38lTU

[3] https://www.epi.org/publication/women-are-more-likely-to-work-multiple-jobs-than-men/

[4] https://www.theguardian.com/world/2019/oct/31/mount-everest-lhakpa-sherpa-climbed-nine-times-world-record

[5] https://leanin.org/women-in-the-workplace-2019?utm_source=newsletter&utm_medium=email&utm_campaign=wiw

[6] Carrie Gracie, *Equal*, Virago, 2019

[7] https://www.theguardian.com/world/2019/oct/14/metoo-two-years-weinstein-allegations-tip-of-iceberg-accusers-zelda-perkins-rosanna-arquette

Chapter Two

[1] Michael Beckwith, author and New Thought Minister—where 'It is what it is—accept it. Harvest the good. Forgive all the rest."

[2] Danielle LaPorte, *White Hot Truth*, Virtuonica, 2017

[3] Words of the Wild Side

[4] https://www.telegraph.co.uk/news/2020/01/19/third-girls-say-have-sexually-harassed-school-charity-survey/

[5] https://www.theguardian.com/society/2020/jan/19/girls-struggle-to-find-safe-place-in-uk-plan-international-report

[6]https://www.womensaid.org.uk/what-we-do/campaigning-and-influencing/femicide-census/

[7]Caroline Criado Perez, *Invisible Women*, Chatto & Windus, 2019

[8]https://www.habitatforhumanity.org.uk/country/brazil/

[9]https://www.nsvrc.org/node/4737

[10]https://rapecrisis.org.uk/get-informed/about-sexual-violence/statistics-sexual-violence/

[11]Katty Kay & Claire Shipman, *The Confidence Code*, Harper Collins Business, 2014

Chapter Three

[1]Caroline Perez Criado, *Invisible Women*, Chatto & Windus, 2019

Chapter Four

[1]https://www.lifehack.org/285774/10-signs-truly-confident-people

Chapter Five

[1] https://en.unesco.org/gem-report/sites/gem-report/files/girls-factsheet-en.pdf

[2]https://ourworldindata.org/how-many-children-are-not-in-school

[3] Bob Proctor, *It's Not About the Money*, G&D Media, 2018

[4]https://www.youtube.com/watch?v=jbUp6CMnTqQ

[5]https://www.youtube.com/watch?v=vwSRqaZGsPw

Chapter Six

[1] https://selfpublishingadvice.org/history-of-self-publishing/

[2] https://www.ingramspark.com/blog/self-publishing-trends-2018-2019

[3] https://publishingperspectives.com/2011/05/200-million-americans-want-to-publish-books/

[4] Inman, 2016

[5] https://hbr.org/2013/09/global-rise-of-female-entrepreneurs

[6] https://www.forbes.com/sites/stephaniesarkis/2019/03/05/gender-inequality-led-to-the-rise-of-women-entrepreneurs/

Chapter Seven

[1] http://www.businessdictionary.com/definition/performance.html

Chapter Nine

[1] Danielle LaPorte, *White Hot Truth*, Virtuonica, 2017

[2] https://georgiavarjas.com/

ABOUT THE AUTHOR

Georgia Varjas is a women's leadership specialist, blogger, author and speaker, who empowers and encourages women to step up and stand out so that they can be heard, understood, and ultimately believed.

A multi-book author and blogger, Georgia has written almost 200 blogs about women empowerment and feminist issues. *The Rule Breakers Guide* was published in July 2020.

Georgia is uniquely placed within the women's leadership field bringing to it energy, confidence, and wisdom which stems from her 25-year career as a musician, performance poet, playwright and author.

She has received publicity in leading media outlets such as *BBC Radio, Glamour, and Thrive Global* as well as online sites and magazines including *Finance Monthly, Honest Mums, Female First, Soul & Spirit, and Working Mums.*

http://www.georgiavarjas.com